The Tassajara Bread Book

The Tassajara Bread Book

REVISED AND UPDATED EDITION

Edward Espe Brown

SHAMBHALA
Boston & London
1986

SHAMBHALA PUBLICATIONS, INC.
Horticultural Hall
300 Massachusetts Avenue
Boston, Massachusetts 02115

10   9   8   7   6   5   4   3
Redesigned and revised 1986
Printed in the United States of America
Distributed in the United States by Random House
and in Canada by Random House of Canada Ltd.

LIBRARY OF CONGRESS CATALOGING-IN-PUBLICATION DATA
Brown, Edward Espe.
   The Tassajara bread book.

   Includes index.
   1. Bread.   I. Title.
TX769.B83   1985   641.8′15   85-2462
ISBN 0-87773-343-0 (pbk.)
ISBN 0-394-74196-X (Random House: pbk.)

Book Design: Dede Cummings
Illustrations: Frances Thompson and Kent Rush

Dedicated
with respect and appreciation
to all my teachers
past, present, and future:
gods, men, and demons;
beings, animate and inanimate,
living and dead, alive and dying.

Rock and water
wind and tree
bread dough rising

Vastly all
are patient with me.

We need more cooks,
not more cookbooks.

CHARLES V. W. BROOKS

Bread makes itself, by your kindness, with your help, with imagination streaming through you, with dough under hand, you are breadmaking itself, which is why breadmaking is so fulfilling and rewarding.

Recipes do not belong to anyone—given to me, I give them to you. Recipes are only a guide, a skeletal framework, to be fleshed out according to your nature and desire. Your life, your love, will bring these recipes into full creation. This cannot be taught. You already know. So plunge in: cook, love, feel, create. Actualize breadmaking itself.

Working in the Kitchen

What is it, closer than close?
Not impervious or distant, not
stiff or unresponsive. A get-down-
in-the-mud mind, a root-around-
in-the-weeds mind: Food comes
alive with your presence, reaching
out, laboring, taking the time
for flour, salt, water, yeast
to come together, for a bowl
that breaks, the dirty dishes,
a leaky faucet, always more
to cooking than meets the eye!
Each thing asking to be seen, heard,
known, loved, a companion in the dark.
"Take care of the food," it is said,
"as though it was your own eyesight,"
not saying, oh that's all right, we
have plenty, we can throw that away.
Table, teapot, measuring cups, spoons:
the body within the body, the place
where everything connects.
Ripe, succulent fruit, leaves, stems,
roots, seeds: the innermost mind
awakening, fully manifesting. What
are you up to, after all? What is
a way of life that is satisfying,
fulfilling, sustaining and sustainable?
Cups, glasses, sponges, one
body with a hundred faces,
a sticky honey jar, the half-
empty cup of coffee, each asking
to fulfill, each offering the touch
of the beloved.
Enter, plunge into the heart
of the matter: an unknown destination,

an unknown adventure unfolding
with your wits about you and your
not-so-wits. Things emerging in life,
Life emerging in things, no separation.
Concentrating on food, concentrating on
myself, with heart opening, hands offering,
may everything be deliciously full
of warmth and kindness.
Coming from the earth, coming from the air,
a cool breeze, a spark, a flame, go ahead:
Cook, offer yourself, hold nothing back.
Cooking is not like you expected, not like
you anticipated. What is happening is unheard
of, never before experienced. You cook. No mistakes.
You might do it differently next time, but
you did it this way this time. Things
are as they are, even if you say too much this
too little that. And if you want things to stay
the same, remind yourself they have no unchanging nature.
"Wherever you go, remember, there you are." O.K.?
Go ahead. Keep moving. Watch your step.

Contents

Introduction to Revised and Updated Edition   3
Introduction to the First Edition   5
How Could I Have Ever Known (It Would Be Like This)?   6
Ingredients   7
Utensils   11
About Yeast   12

DETAILED INSTRUCTIONS FOR MAKING TASSAJARA
  YEASTED BREAD   *13*

  Mixing Up the Sponge   *16*
  Setting the Dough to Rise   *18*
  Advantages of the Sponge Method   *18*
  Folding in Oil, Salt, and Dry Ingredients   *20*
  Kneading the Dough   *20*
  Rising and Punching the Dough   *26*
  Shaping the Loaves   *26*
  Prebaking and Baking   *29*
  Storing   *29*
  Rolls and Other Shapes   *30*
  Fruit-Filled Loaves   *32*

YEASTED BREADS   *33*

  1   Tassajara Yeasted Bread   *36*
  2   Rye-Oatmeal Bread   *38*
  3   Sesame Bread   *38*
  4   White Egg Bread   *39*
  5   Potato Bread   *39*
  6   Summer Swedish Rye Bread   *40*
  7   Cornmeal-Millet Bread   *40*
  8   Oatmeal Bread   *41*
  9   Millet Bread   *41*
 10   Banana Sandwich Bread   *42*

11 Cinnamon Raisin Bread   *42*

12 Nut or Seed Bread   *43*

13 Fruit Bread   *43*

14 Cheese Bread   *43*

15 A French Bread   *44*

16 Ricotta Olive Bolso   *44*

17 Focaccio   *46*

18 Egg Wash   *46*

YEASTED PASTRIES   *47*

19 Yeasted Breakfast Bread Dough   *49*

20 Swedish Tea Ring   *50*

21 Powdered Sugar Glaze   *51*

22 Cinnamon Rolls   *53*

23 Pecan Nut Rolls   *54*

24 English Muffins   *54*

25 Lemon Twist Bread   *55*

26 Norwegian Coffee Cake   *58*

27 Kolaches   *59*

Kolache Toppings and Fillings   *60*

Poppy Seed Topping   *60*

Butter Glaze   *60*

Prune or Apricot Filling   *60*

Almond Paste   *60*

Date Almond Filling   *61*

28 Braided Christmas Bread   *61*

UNYEASTED BREADS   *63*

29 Tibetan Barley Bread   *66*

30 Overnight Unyeasted Bread I   *66*

31 Overnight Unyeasted Bread II   *67*

32 Unyeasted Dutch Rye Bread   *68*

33 Gruel Bread   *68*

SOURDOUGH BREADS & PANCAKES   *71*

34 Sourdough Bread   *73*

35 Sourdough Rye Bread   *74*

36 Sourdough French Loaves   74
37 Sourdough Pancakes   75
38 Country French Bread   76
39 Sourdough Raisin Rolls   77

PANCAKES & OTHER THINGS TO EAT FOR BREAKFAST, LUNCH, OR DINNER   79

40 Whole Wheat Pancakes   81
41 Orange Whole Wheat Hotcakes   82
42 O-Konomi-Yaki   83
43 Cottage Cheese Pancakes   83
44 Popovers   84
45 Apple Pancake Sam   84
46 Cream Scones   85
47 Flaky Biscuits   86
48 Basil and Parmesan Cheese Flaky Biscuits   87
49 Butter Kuchen   88
50 Egg Bagels   89
51 Walnut Coffee Cake   90

MUFFINS & QUICK BREADS   91

52 Jalapeño Corn Bread   94
53 Three-Layer Corn Bread   94
54 Blue Cornmeal Muffins   95
55 Whole Wheat Muffins   96
56 Something Missing Muffins   96
57 Festival Spice Muffins   97
58 "Oriental" Spice Muffins   98
59 Fruit Juice Muffins   98
60 Marmalade or Jam Muffins   98
61 Dried Fruit Muffins   98
62 Nut or Seed Muffins   99
63 Confusion Muffins   99
64 Corn Muffins   100
65 Bran Muffins   100
66 Barley Flour Muffins   101
67 Carrot Cake   102
68 Apple Nut Loaf (Yeasted)   103

69 Banana Nut Bread   *104*
70 Honey Walnut Bread   *104*
71 Date Nut Bread   *105*

COMPOUND BUTTERS   *107*

Nut Butters   *109*
72 Hazelnut Butter   *110*
73 Almond and Orange Butter   *110*
74 Pecan and Ginger Butter   *110*
Sweet Butters   *111*
75 Honey Lemon Butter   *111*
76 Chocolate Nutmeg Butter   *111*
77 Vanilla Bean Butter   *111*
78 Coffee Liqueur Butter   *112*
Savory Butters   *113*
79 Balsamic Butter   *113*
80 Lemon Mustard Butter   *113*
81 Lime and Cilantro Butter   *114*
82 Roasted Garlic and Hot Chili Butter   *114*

DESSERTS   *115*

83 Cheesecake Cookies   *118*
84 Turkish Coffee Cake Cookie Bars   *119*
85 Honey Bars   *120*
86 Date Bars   *121*
87 Tassajara Shortbread   *122*
88 Lemon Bars   *122*
89 Walnut Cookies   *123*
90 Italian Cookies   *124*
91 Coconut Macaroons   *124*
92 Nutty Gritty Cookies   *125*
93 Fresh Fruit Cake   *126*
94 Haver Cookies   *127*
95 Sesame Candy (Halvah)   *128*
96 Raw Fruit Carob Candy   *128*

 97 Cream Cheese Balls   *129*
 98 Apple Crisp   *130*
 99 Peach Kuchen   *131*
100 Torte with Sour Cream Fruit Topping   *132*
101 Mustard Gingerbread   *133*
102 Yogurt Cake   *134*
103 Triple Chocolate Cake   *134*
104 Simple Chocolate Glaze   *135*
105 Chocolate Glaze   *136*
106 White Layer Cake or Boston Cream Pie   *136*
107 Vanilla Pastry Cream   *137*
108 Buttercream Frosting   *138*
109 Cream Cheese Icing   *138*
110 Chocolate Mousse Pie   *139*
111 Short Pastry for Tarts   *141*
112 Fresh Fruit Tart   *142*
113 Fresh Fruit Cheesecake Tart   *143*

About Ed Brown   144
Acknowledgments   145
About Tassajara   146

The Tassajara Bread Book

Introduction to Revised and Updated Edition

Fifteen years have passed since *The Tassajara Bread Book* first appeared. During that time I have heard from numerous people how much they appreciated this book: made bread for the first time, enjoyed it, felt the mysterious way in which the simple activity of breadmaking was fulfilling and rewarding, a profound expression of caring, of nurturing oneself and others. As one woman put it, she experienced a "silent, hidden, quiet revolution" taking place in the kitchen and her heart.

The heart's work is to open, to absorb the pain and respond, according to the circumstances. What an immense task sometimes just to continue in the face of the pain: a frown, a scowl, an angry word; children dying of cancer, children missing, murdered, killed in automobile accidents; bombs a few minutes away. Often I wonder, "How can I help? What can I do?" What a gift that in the midst of the suffering one can find simple ways of expressing warmth and kindness. As I mention in the introduction to Christmas Braided Bread, my grandmother lived long enough to see her husband and all but one of her children die— and went on baking bread.

Also in the fifteen years since this book was first printed, we have seen the appearance of many more bakers, many more bakeries, and many more books on bread. Unbleached white flour has made it to the supermarket shelves. Small changes, maybe, but I am happy and grateful to have played a small part with the writing of this book.

I know of one group in Bloomington, Indiana, who opened a bakery, using *The Tassajara Bread Book* as its guide. Three of them would knead the bread by hand in a huge mixing bowl, until one day a real baker showed up and laughed at what he saw. He couldn't believe it. They studied with him, worked at it, kept learning, stayed with it (leaving the *Bread Book* far behind). Soon they had seven retail stores and a large bakery *plant*. In 1976 when we started our retail bakery, The Tassajara Bread Bakery, in San Francisco, we had no experience baking in quantity like that. Some folks from Indiana came to advise us. Back and forth the energy, knowledge, and inspiration flow. Thank goodness, I do not have to dream up everything myself.

Numerous people worked to make our bakery successful. Peter Overton and Doug Volkmer in particular established a tradition which others have carried on, enlarged, adapted, altered. The new recipes in this revised edition are not something I made up. I went to our bakery and they were kind enough to share some of their recipes with me. Now I pass them on. Our lives are intimately connected, inextricably bound together. We work to feed each other.

A second source of new recipes has been a friend who lives down the hill, Sammie Daniels. She is responsible for the section on compound butters. We also worked together reducing the bakery recipes to home scale, testing them out in the baking and the eating. I am very grateful for her help, sharing this task with me.

I am not a great baker, and I do not promise that you will become a superbaker by using this book. That is not the point. I do not bake to be great. I bake because it is wholesome. I feel renewed, and I am renewing the world, my friends and neighbors. Most of us bake in this way.

Someone told me recently that learning how to bake bread from my book was like regaining his life from corporate America. "A rite of passage," he said, "an initiation," a reconnection with the earth, our roots, our common heritage, our shared life and livelihood. So be it.

Please carry on—the work of feeding, the work of the heart. Bread, I realized, cannot live by words alone. What you knead is what you get. And if that is too cute or clever, put it down and go on to something else. And thank you for your effort.

Introduction to the First Edition

Breadmaking is basically not a complicated process. Mix some flour with enough water to form a dough, adding a touch of salt perhaps; shape it, bake it, the result is bread in its simplest, most fundamental form: dense, coarse, crusty, robust, spirited, earthy.

Everything else (in a way) is extra: yeast, to make it lighter; milk, to give a softer crumb; sugar or honey to sweeten it; oil, for moistness; eggs, for cakiness. The extras make bread more palatable, more pleasing, more chewable and sliceable. The extras provide surprise and delight. Still, there is something to be said for primitive simplicity, for tasting the true spirit of the wheat.

So I give you a choice of a variety of recipes, from the unyeasted flour-salt-water breads to the yeasted pastries using butter, eggs, milk, and sugar. Take your pick, and put some time into it: you and the dough—ripening, maturing, baking, blossoming together.

How Could I Have Ever Known
(It Would Be Like This)?

While we worked together in the garden, a friend told me, "Flowers are angels from distant stars come down to earth with their heavenly message. The more time you spend with them, the more you touch them, tend them, sit with them, regard them, the more you hear their message."

"And what do you listen with?" I asked.

"You listen with your eyes and nose, hands and ears."

"And what about the cheeks? Is it not a whole body listening?"

"Yes, a whole body listening."

What to do, how to tend, how to pass on the message: star food, angel food, transfixed body, body of light, food body, cooking body. Body of bread, cake-body, body of biscuits, seed-body: the Heart of Compassion enters the truth of the moment, listening, hearing, responding.

When I cook, another body comes alive. Not the body of walking or typing, not the body of sitting or talking, but the body of cooking: a body alive to flavors and fragrance, a body ready to touch and be touched, a body which eats with eyes as well as mouth, eats and is eaten. Hands awaken, boundless with their own knowledge, picking up, handling, putting down. A whole body, nothing but food, offering.

This body cooking is also the body of my child, the body of my parents. A body holding my daughter, a body being held. Taking your tiny hand in mine, your first day of school, we walk slowly knowing life will never be the same again, and this moment is precious. My hand in yours as I breathe one last breath, nothing left to accomplish, no one left to please, I let go and relax. No one tied down, no one to be freed. No more worry about not being perfect. What's for breakfast?

Ingredients

Love is not only the most important ingredient:
it is the only ingredient which really matters.

—from a cookbook by a British chef

The ingredients listed are mostly "whole" foods. This "wholeness" means that the flour, meal (a coarser grind than flour), or flakes contain all the elements of the whole grain, particularly the "germ," that part of the grain kernel from which the grain would sprout if planted. So this germ is the most life-containing, life-giving part of the grain. Studies show this in terms of its being higher in vitamins and essential oils than other parts of the grain.

For this reason "whole" cornmeal, which contains the germ, will have a greater life-containing, life-giving quality than the "degermed" cornmeal found in supermarkets. Whole cornmeal is a "live" food—it spoils when the oil in the germ becomes rancid. Degermed cornmeal is a "dead" food, as it lacks the germ (of life). Hence, it can be kept on grocery shelves for months without spoiling, though like all milled grains it does become stale.

In any case, best to buy grain products as freshly milled as possible and to preserve their freshness by refrigerating them in sealed jars or plastic bags. But don't let a lack of whole grain products keep you from making bread. Most of the recipes can be made with regular white flour, if necessary.

Whole wheat flour provides the basic foundation of bread. With a deep, full-flavored, hearty wheat taste, it contains all the elements of the wheat kernel: flour, bran, and germ. The bran and germ have good amounts of B vitamins. Stoneground whole wheat flour has a fresher taste and higher nutritional properties than flour produced from high-speed milling, because of the lower temperatures of stone grinding. Wheat flour contains the highest amount of gluten, a substance that holds air in the dough and expands like hundreds of small balloons, giving dough its elasticity. For this reason most of the bread recipes include at least one-half whole wheat or unbleached white flour.

Unbleached white flour is mechanically refined to remove the bran and germ, has not been chemically treated, and contains no preserving chemicals. Compared with the standard all-purpose bleached white flours, it has a distinctly "live" taste. The high gluten content of white flour makes it particularly useful in breadmaking. Small amounts of this flour (10%) give lightness and increased workability to bread doughs. If bread dough is too heavy or too sticky, add more white flour next time. Use it also for special occasions and particular recipes that are lighter and more delicate.

Rye flour contains less gluten than wheat does and tends to produce a fine-textured, moist, dense bread. Small amounts (10%–15%) add smoothness and workability to doughs with a high proportion of granular ingredients, such as corn–rye, rye–oatmeal. Large amounts of rye flour tend to produce a sticky dough.

Cornmeal gives breads a more crumbly texture, a crunchiness and sweetness. *Whole* cornmeal, though it spoils more readily, is superior in taste and nutriment to the degermed cornmeal found in supermarkets. Meal is a coarser grind than flour.

Millet meal, though somewhat bland-tasting, adds a surprising crunchy richness to breads.

Rolled oats make bread chewy, moist, sweet. Their white flakes often make a beautiful mosaic in molasses-darkened breads. To make rolled oats, as distinct from oatmeal, whole oat kernels are pressed flat between rollers. Oatmeal has most often been subjected to a greater amount of processing. Oats are the grain richest in minerals, salt, fat, and protein.

Barley flour is particularly delicious in breads if pan-toasted before being added to the bread dough. As such it gives breads a sweet, moist, cakelike quality.

Brown rice flour is sweet and will tend to make bread moist, dense, and smooth. Cooked brown rice gives bread a moist, chewy character.

Buckwheat flour has a very distinctive taste and, while tending to make bread heavy, it is "full" of warmth—a good winter food.

Whole grains and cracked grains should be cooked before being added to bread. When you use cooked grains, less water or more flour will be necessary.

Yeast is a microscopic fungus that, as a by-product of its existence, makes bread rise. All yeasted recipes use dry baker's yeast.

Milk makes bread smoother, softer, and more cakelike, and modifies, masks the "coarse" grain taste. Recipes call for dry milk, though whole milk can be used if scalded (heated to just below boiling) and then cooled to lukewarm. This has to do with killing various enzymes which would otherwise interfere with the activity of the yeast.

Eggs will make bread lighter, more airy, and tender and will give a golden color.

Oil makes a richer-tasting, cakier bread. Nonhydrogenated liquid vegetable oils are more readily digested and usefully assimilated by the body than hydrogenated (solidified or hardened) oils such as shortening and margarine, though the use of these hardened oils tends to make a flakier dough.

"Cold-pressed" oils are likely to be higher in essential fatty acids than regular commercial oils. Even so, most cold-pressed oils are highly refined, so that they are clear, light, and nearly colorless. Oils in their more raw state are cloudy and tend to smell strongly of the plant of derivation. Also they are more *oily*.

Once again it is a question of commercial value as opposed to human welfare. Those oils which are more highly refined and processed will keep better (often with the use of preservatives) and are "purer," so they are more practical for shipping, storing, and selling to a public that generally prefers the cheaper, "sanitized" product.

Sweetenings tend to stimulate the appetite (more, more). Honey or molasses is used in most recipes calling for sweetening, though in some cases their use is impractical. "Unfiltered, unblended, uncooked" honey contains more enzymes and minerals than regular commercial honey. Molasses, particularly blackstrap molasses, contains valuable amounts of B vitamins and minerals, including iron. Blackstrap does have a distinctive, strong taste. Honey or molasses will make the bread pleasantly fragrant as well as sweet. Sugar, particularly white sugar, has a noted lack of nutritive factors aside from calories. This tends to create an overabundance of sugar in the body, eventually resulting in lowered blood sugar or less energy.

Dates or raisins or other dried fruits may also replace some of the sweetening.

Salt will give its unique benefits. Sea salt or unrefined salt contains numerous trace elements often lacking in the usual diet.

Carob flour is used in some of the recipes. Carob has a naturally sweet taste similar to chocolate. It is very wholesome, well-balanced, readily digestible food containing good amounts of B vitamins, vitamin A, minerals, and protein, as opposed to chocolate, which is not noted as a balanced food, capable of being a dietary staple. For special occasions, however, chocolate does provide satisfaction and pleasure unobtainable from carob.

Utensils

Certain items will assist you in making bread, though few of them are strictly necessary. *Heavy brown ceramic bread bowls* are available. These hold and distribute heat well, which helps the bread dough rise. Preheating the bowl allows the baby bread dough to feel at home and warmly held. A *stainless steel bread bowl* won't break. Large pots, clean buckets, or a plastic basin can provide a home for your doughs. *Mixing spoons, wood or metal, a set of measuring spoons, a 1-cup* and a *2-cup measure* are useful, along with a *rubber spatula* for cleaning cups and bowls. But, if necessary, you *can* do all the measuring and mixing with your hands. Most of the recipes are approximations anyway to give you *some* idea. Learn to feel for yourself, through experience and experimentation.

A *good-sized bread board* for kneading is something worth taking good care of. Use it only for breads. Don't cut on it, and store it in a clean, dry place. Keep it clean and dry. A wet towel between the board and the table will keep it from slipping while in use. Kneading right on the table is all right, too, if you keep it carefully cleaned. A table approximately at the height at which your hands rest comfortably allows ease in kneading. Give yourself plenty of clear open space to work in.

Bread pans, sometimes aluminum and rectangular; 5¼ by 9¼ and 4½ by 8½ inches are standard sizes. For small loaves, use pans 3¾ by 7½ inches. Wash them only once a year, and they will develop dark tempering. The bread will bake faster and not stick. Other possibilities include *cookie sheets, metal cups, glass or enamel pans, small ceramic flowerpots;* let their shape be the shape of your breads. An *oven for baking*, although you can always make any bread into English muffins or crackers if you have a griddle or a frying pan and stove or fire.

About Yeast

To wait on yeast is to feed, keep house, keep it warm, clean its air, empty its garbage, and cater to its whims. Getting angry at its failings does not help. Providing patient, loving care and food for growth does. Begin by dissolving the dry yeast in lukewarm water 90° to 105° F. At temperatures much higher than 105°, the yeast becomes very frantically active and soon exhausts itself; at lower temperatures it lives a more dormant existence, until below freezing, it barely respirates.

Most bread recipes say, "Dissolve the yeast in ¼ cup lukewarm water. Scald milk. . . ." This method does of course produce excellent results (and I include some of those recipes here); however, it is sufficient and timely to dissolve the yeast in the entire amount of water and then stir in the powdered milk, in which case the milk need not be scalded.

Yeast needs oxygen to breathe and simple sugars to eat. Though some simple sugars are present in flour, because of the action of enzymes on more complex starch molecules, generally some sweetening is added for the yeast to dine on. Treat it to molasses (mild or a little blackstrap); honey (avocado, buckwheat, tupolo, or choice fancy); brown or white sugars; or corn syrup. Living yeast turns the oxygen and sugars into carbon dioxide and alcohols. (Brewer's yeast is an even better alcohol producer.) The carbon dioxide becoming trapped in the glutenous network of dough is what makes the bread rise.

Take care that the carbon dioxide and the alcohols do not build up extensively enough that the yeast suffocates and generally expires in its own wastes. Punching down the dough or otherwise working with it releases gaseous by-products of the yeast existence and freshens its air. Bake the bread, and the yeast dies. Slice it, butter it, eat it. Be thankful.

A note: Dry yeast bought in bulk at a natural foods store costs a fraction of what it costs in those little packets at the supermarket.

Detailed Instructions for Making Tassajara Yeasted Bread

Detailed Instructions for Making Tassajara Yeasted Bread

Yeasted bread is made principally with wheat flour, which is what gives bread its distinctive elastic texture. Other grains do not have the gluten content of wheat, but they can be incorporated into the bread to give variation in texture, taste, and nutriment. Rye, corn, millet, barley, rice, oats, and buckwheat may be used. Further variation of flavor and texture involves the use of milk, eggs, oil, butter, sugar, honey, or molasses. Once the dough is ready for baking, there are many ways to shape and bake it.

The Tassajara Yeasted Bread recipe leads into all the other yeasted bread and pastry recipes: rye–oatmeal, corn–rye, English muffins, cinnamon rolls. Make the basic bread once, and you will be ready to tackle any of the recipes. Give it your time and attention.

Here is an outline of the instructions that follow:

I. *Getting Started*
  A. *Mixing Up the Sponge*
  B. *Setting the Sponge to Rise*
  C. *Advantages of the Sponge Method*

II. *Seeing It to the Finish*
  A. *Folding in Oil, Salt, and Dry Ingredients*
  B. *Kneading the Dough*
  C. *Rising and Punching the Dough*
  D. *Shaping the Loaves*
  E. *Prebaking and Baking*
  F. *Storing*

Mixing Up the Sponge

All measurements are for the basic Tassajara Yeasted Bread, recipe #1.

3 cups lukewarm water (85°–105° F)
1½ tablespoons dry yeast (2 packages)
¼ cup sweetening (honey, molasses, or brown sugar)
1 cup dry milk (optional)
4 cups whole wheat flour (substitute 1 or more cups unbleached white flour if desired)

[Makes 2 loaves]

Measure 3 cups water and put it in a good-sized bowl. "Lukewarm" does not feel warm or cold on your wrist.

Sprinkle the dry baker's yeast over the water and stir to dissolve. For faster rising and lighter bread, use an additional package of yeast (¾ tablespoon).

Add ¼ cup sweetening. You can rinse the measuring cup out in the water if you wish. Two tablespoons of sweetening would be quite sufficient for the growth of the yeast; amounts larger than ¼ cup may be added for sweet tooths.

Add dry milk and stir to dissolve. Complete dissolving is not necessary (Figure 1), as the ingredients will become well mixed when the batter is thicker. The bread will have a grainier taste and a coarser texture if the dry milk is omitted. In this case less flour will be needed.

If eggs are desired (as in some of the variations), beat and add at this stage, adding more flour as needed for proper consistency of the dough. Or the eggs may be added to the completed sponge *after* the flour is in and the batter beaten.

Then add whole wheat flour a cup or so at a time, stirring briskly after each addition (Figure 2). As the mixture thickens, begin beating with a spoon, stirring up and down in small strokes and in circles at the surface of the mixture (Figures 4 and 5). Scrape the sides of the bowl occasionally (Figure 3). After 4 cups of flour have been added, the mixture will be quite thick, but still beatable—a thick mud.

Now beat about 100 times (Figures 4 and 5) until the batter is very smooth. Do this at the surface of the dough, ducking the spoon under

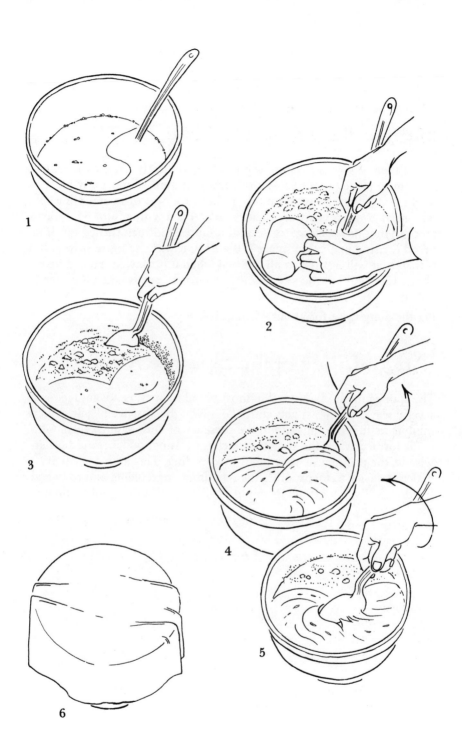

the surface, then bringing it up above the surface, pulling up the batter in a circular motion. The batter will become stretchier as you do this and air will be incorporated into the sponge.

Setting the Dough to Rise

Cover the bowl with a damp towel to keep off draft (Figure 6). Set in a warmish place (about 85°–100°). In the summer almost any place might do. Otherwise set it on top of the stove over or near a pilot light, on a shelf above a hot-water heater, in an oven with a pilot light, or in an oven that has been on for several minutes and then turned off. If the bread is rising in a cooler place (70°–85°), it will rise more slowly. If it is frozen, it will not rise at all but will when it is thawed. Heat above about 120° will kill the yeast, which is what happens when the bread is baked.

Let the dough rise for about 45 minutes.

Advantages of the Sponge Method

The sponge method, omitted in most bread recipes, is advantageous in several ways. The yeast gets started easily in the absence of salt, which inhibits its functioning, and in the presence of abundant oxygen. Gluten is formed when the sponge stretches in rising, which would otherwise be the product of *your* labor in kneading. This added elasticity makes it easier to incorporate the remaining ingredients and to knead the dough. Even a 10- to 15-minute rising at this point will facilitate the remaining steps.

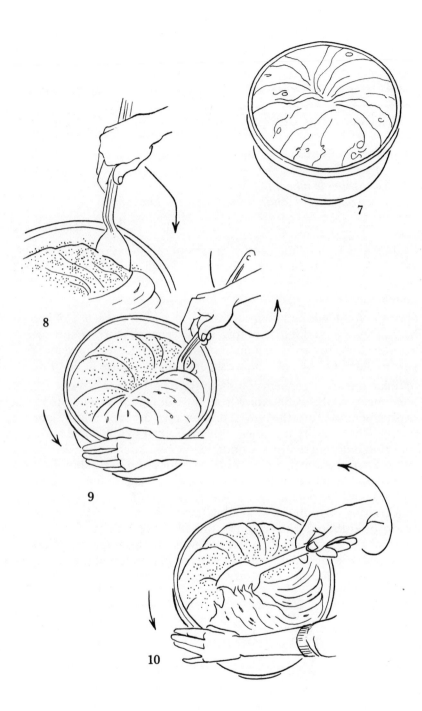

7

8

9

10

Folding in Oil, Salt, and Dry Ingredients

All measurements are for the basic Tassajara Yeasted Bread, recipe #1.

> *4 teaspoons salt*
> *⅓ cup oil (or butter or margarine)*
> *3 cups whole wheat flour*
> *1 cup additional whole wheat flour for kneading*

[Makes 2 loaves]

Folding in is the method used to mix from this point on (Figures 8, 9, 10). *Do not stir.* Do not cut through the dough. Keep it in one piece as much as possible. This will improve the elasticity and strength of the dough.

Sprinkle in the salt and pour on the oil. Stir around the *side* of the bowl (Figure 8) and fold over toward the center (Figures 9 and 10). Turn the bowl toward you a quarter turn with your left hand and repeat folding until oil and salt are incorporated (Figures 8, 9, 10).

Sprinkle the dry ingredients on the surface of the dough about a ½ cup at a time. Fold the wet mixture from the sides of the bowl on top of the dry ingredients. Turn the bowl a quarter turn between folds (Figures 8, 9, 10). When the dry ingredients are moistened by the dough, add some more dry ingredients. Continue folding. After adding 2 cups of wheat flour, the dough will become very thick and heavy, but don't be intimidated. Continue folding in an additional cup of flour (Figures 11 and 12) until the dough comes away from the sides and bottom of the bowl, sitting up in the bowl in a big lump (Figure 12). The dough is ready for kneading when it can be turned out of the bowl in pretty much of a piece, except for a few remaining scraps (Figure 13). Take time to scrape the bowl, and lay the scrapings on top of the dough on a floured board. It is not necessary to wash the bread bowl at this point; just oil it lightly.

Kneading the Dough

The kneading surface, a board or a tabletop, should be at a height on which your hands rest comfortably when you are standing straight. You need to be able to exert some downward pressure. Keep the surface

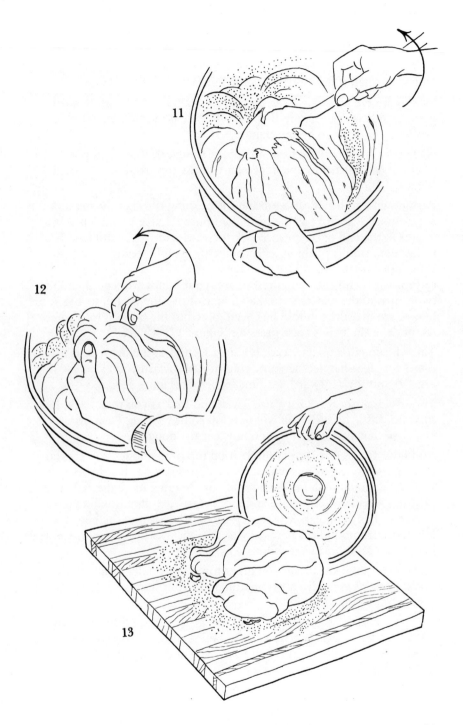

floured enough to prevent the dough from sticking during kneading. The purpose of kneading is to get the dough well mixed, give it a smooth, even texture, and further develop its elasticity.

Flour your hands and sprinkle some flour on top of the dough.

Picking up the far edge of the dough, fold the dough in half toward you, far side over near side (Figure 14), so that the two edges are approximately lined up evenly (Figure 15).

Place your hands on the near side of the dough so that the top of your palms (just below the fingers) are at the top front of the dough (Figure 15).

Push down and forward, centering the pushing through the heels of the hands more and more as the push continues (Figure 16). Relax your fingers at the end of the push. Rock forward with your whole body rather than simply pushing with your arms. Apply steady, even pressure, allowing the dough to give way at its own pace. The dough will roll forward with the seam on top, and your hands will end up about two-thirds of the way toward the far side of the dough. Removing your hands, see that the top fold has been joined to the bottom fold where the heels of the hands were pressing (Figure 17).

Turn the dough a quarter turn (Figures 18 and 19); clockwise is usually easier for right-handed persons. Fold in half toward you as before (Figure 19) and rock forward, pushing as before (Figure 16).

Turn, fold, push. Rock forward. Twist and fold as you rock back. Rock forward. Little by little you will develop some rhythm. Push firmly yet gently so that you stretch but do not tear the dough.

Add flour to the board or sprinkle it on top of the dough as necessary to keep the dough from sticking to the board or your hands. As you knead, the dough will begin stiffening up, holding its shape rather than sagging; it will become more and more elastic, so that it will tend to stretch rather than tear. It will stick to your hands and the board less and less until no flour is necessary to prevent sticking. The surface will be smooth and somewhat shiny.

As you continue kneading, you may stop occasionally to scrape the bread board (Figure 20) and rub dough off your hands, and incorporate these scraps into the dough.

When you are finished kneading, place the dough (Figure 21) in the oiled bread bowl smooth side down, and then turn it over so the creases are on the bottom (Figure 22). The oiled surface will keep a crust from forming on the dough.

Cover the dough with a damp towel and set it in a warm place.

14

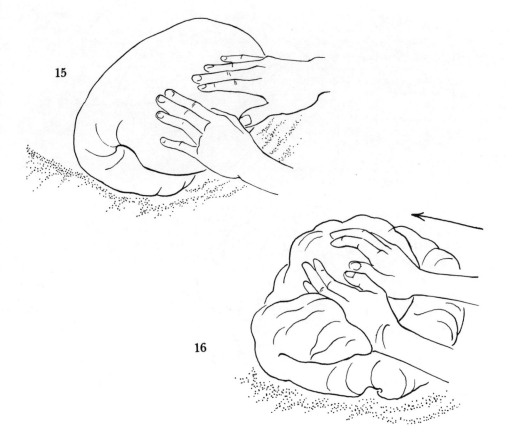

15

16

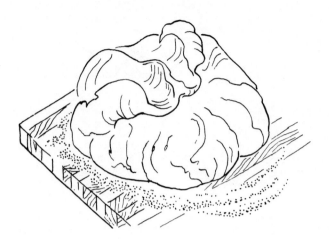

17

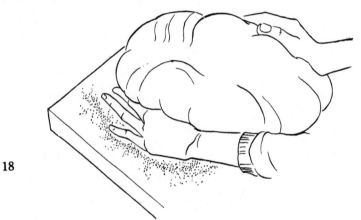

18

19

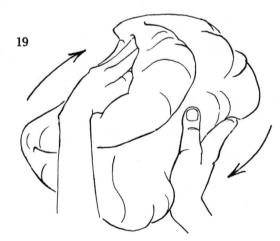

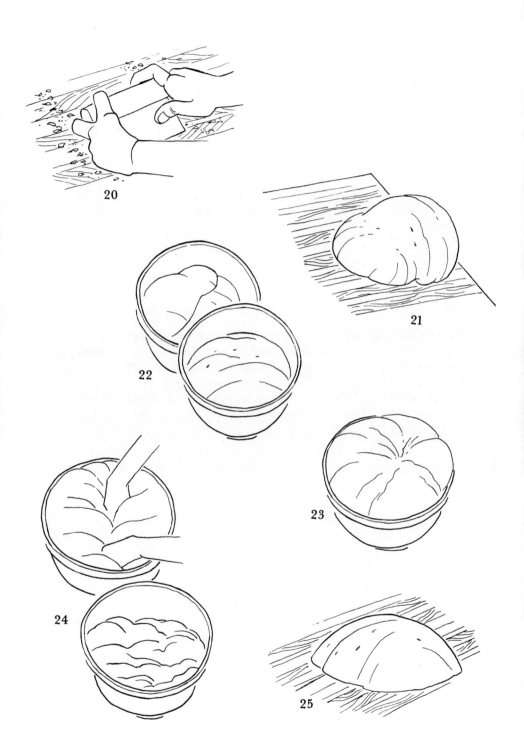

Rising and Punching the Dough

Let the dough rise 50–60 minutes, until nearly doubled in size (Figure 23).

"Punch down" by pushing your fist into the dough, as far as it will go, steadily and firmly. Do this maybe fifteen or twenty times all over the dough (Figure 24). It will not punch down as small as it was before rising. Cover.

Let rise 40–50 minutes, until nearly doubled in size. If you are short for time, the second rising may be omitted. The loaves will be slightly denser.

Shaping the Loaves

Start the oven preheating. (Adjustment of oven temperature may be necessary. Electric ovens, especially, should probably be set 25° lower than indicated temperature.) Turn the dough onto the board (Figure 25). If it is of the proper consistency (i.e., moisture content), you won't need flour on the board. If it is too wet, it will stick on the board. Use flour as necessary. If it is too dry, the folds will not seal together easily.

Shape the dough into a ball by folding it to the center all the way around (Figure 26) as in kneading without the pushing (Figure 27). Turn smooth side up, and tuck in the dough all the way around (Figure 28).

Cut into two even pieces (Figure 29). Shape each piece into a ball, and let them sit for 5 minutes.

For each loaf, knead the dough with your right hand (Figure 30). Turn and fold it with your left hand (Figure 31). Do this about five or six times until dough is compact. This gives the loaf added "spring," similar to winding a clock. After the final push, turn the dough a quarter turn.

Beginning at the near edge, roll up the dough into a log shape (Figure 32). With the seam on the bottom, flatten out the top with your fingertips (Figure 33). Square off the sides and ends (Figure 34). Turn the dough over and pinch the seams together all the way along it (Figure 35).

Have bread pans in a stack. Put some oil in the top one and turn it over, letting it drain into the next one (Figure 36). Place a loaf in the

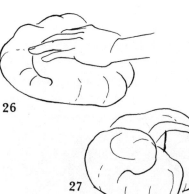

26

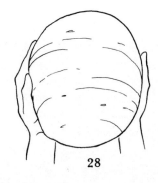

28

27

29

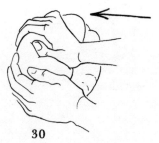

30

31

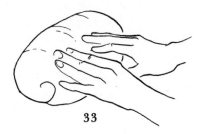

32

33

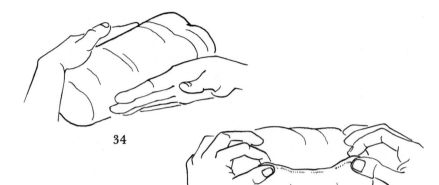

34

35

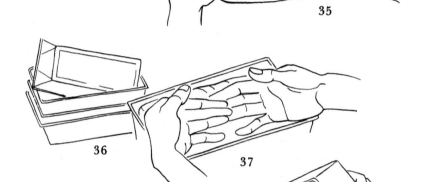

36

37

38

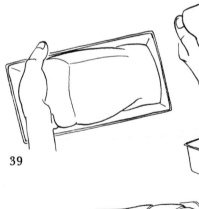

39

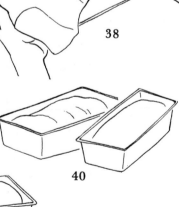

40

41

oiled pan with the seam up. The dough can fill the pan one-half to two-thirds full. A 4½- by 8½-inch pan will make a loaf smaller but higher than a 5¼- by 9¼-inch pan.

Flatten the dough with the backs of your fingers (Figure 37). Turn the loaf over so that the seam is on the bottom (Figures 38 and 39). Press it again into the shape of the pan with the backs of your fingers (Figure 37).

Cover. Let rise 20–25 minutes from the time you finished the last loaf, depending partly on how long you take to make the loaves and partly on how fast the dough is rising. The center of the loaf will be at or close to the top of the pan by this time (Figure 40).

Prebaking and Baking

Cut the top with slits ½ inch deep to allow steam to escape (Figure 41). For a golden brown, shiny surface, brush the surface with egg wash: 1 egg beaten with 2 tablespoons water or milk.

Sprinkle with sesame seeds or poppy seeds if you wish.

Bake at 350° for 50–60 minutes. (Smaller loaves will bake faster.) When done, the top should be shiny golden brown, the sides and bottoms should also be golden brown, and the loaf will resound with a hollow thump when tapped with a finger.

Remove from pans immediately. For clean-cut slices, let cool one hour or more before cutting.

Storing

When completely cooled, bread may be kept in a sealed plastic bag in the refrigerator. Finished bread may also be frozen and thawed for later use, with slight impairment of flavor and freshness. Somewhat stale bread may be freshened by heating in a 350° oven for 10–15 minutes. Dry bread can still be used for toast or French toast, croutons, or bread crumbs.

For zweiback, cut dry bread into cubes and rebake at 200° until crunchy and dry.

Rolls and Other Shapes

Though they are usually made from a dough rich with butter and eggs, rolls can also be made from any bread dough. If short for time before a meal, you may wish to take advantage of the fact that rolls bake more quickly than bread and can be served immediately out of the oven, whereas bread must cool before it can be well sliced.

Figure on 12–15 rolls per loaf of bread dough.

GENERAL DIRECTIONS FOR ROLLS

Form into a log shape about one loaf's worth of bread dough; the log should be 1½–2 inches in diameter (Figure 42) and is formed by rolling the dough between your hands and the bread board.

Section the log into equal-sized pieces (Figure 43).

Shape it into one or more of the following types of rolls or some other shape.

Let rise 20 minutes.

Apply egg wash (and sprinkle with poppy or sesame seeds).

Bake about 25 minutes at 375° until nicely browned.

Plain Rolls (the simplest and plainest)
Place the sectioned pieces on edge or flat on a greased sheet or a sheet sprinkled with cornmeal (Figure 44).

Clover Leaf Rolls
Divide sections into three pieces. Shape each into a ball. Place three balls in a greased muffin cup (Figures 45 and 49).

Snail or Spiral Rolls
Roll each section into a length about 6 inches long. Coil it up and place in a greased muffin cup (Figures 46, 47, 49).

Flower Rolls
Roll each section into a length 8 inches long. Fold double, end to end, and twist. Then coil it and place it in a greased muffin cup (Figures 48 and 49).

Butterhorn or Crescent
Do not shape the dough into a log. Roll it out in a circle about ¼ inch thick. Brush with melted butter or margarine. Cut into 8–12 wedges. Roll it up, starting from the wide end. Twist to form a crescent. Place crescent on greased sheet (Figure 50).

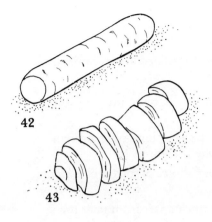

42

43

44

45

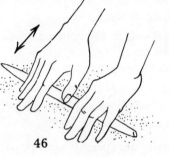

46

47

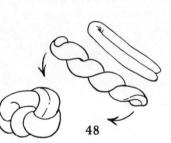

48

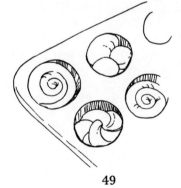

49

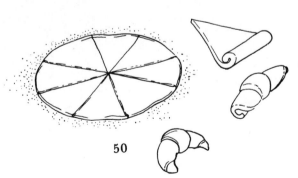

50

Fruit-Filled Loaves

Any yeasted bread dough can be made into fruit-filled loaves braided on top. Make any size loaf.

Flatten dough into a rectangle about ½ inch thick by rolling, pressing, and/or stretching (Figure 51).

Arrange sliced fruit pieces (apple, banana, peach, plum, pear, apricot, nectarine) down the center third of the dough (Figure 52).

Sprinkle on brown sugar if you like and your choice of spices: cinnamon, allspice, nutmeg, mace, anise.

Make diagonal cuts in the dough about ½ inch apart from near the fruit out to the edge.

Fold the strips alternately over the fruit, stretching and twisting slightly to form a compact loaf (Figure 52).

Place loaf in a baking pan or on a greased baking sheet.

Let rise 20 minutes.

Apply egg wash (and sprinkle with poppy seeds).

Bake 350° for one hour or until golden brown.

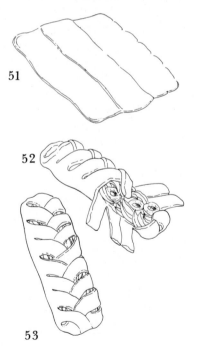

51

52

53

Yeasted Breads

Yeasted Breads

The first recipe is a basic one that offers ample opportunity for variation and experimentation. This is the yeasted bread that visitors to Tassajara Zen Mountain Center have come to know and enjoy, the bread that hundreds of people take home with them each summer.

Now you can make it yourself and invent your own variations. You can have the aroma of freshly baked bread in your kitchen. Nothing is difficult about this recipe, as there is a wide margin for error, adaptation, and experimentation. If you have never made bread, your first batch is going to be better than nothing. After that, no comparison! Each batch is unique and full of your sincere effort. Offer it forth.

Now that fifteen years have passed since this book first came out, I can say that I have heard over and over again from people that they could finally make bread—following the basic recipe and the "Detailed Instructions"—after never having been able to before.

I Tassajara Yeasted Bread

The basic Tassajara yeasted bread recipe, from which all of the others
follow. (For further explanation of the directions, see "Detailed Instructions for Making Tassajara Yeasted Bread," page 15.)

I.   *3 cups lukewarm water (85°–105°F)*
     1½ tablespoons dry yeast (2 packages)
     ¼ cup sweetening (honey, molasses, or brown sugar)
     1 cup dry milk (optional)
     4 cups whole wheat flour (substitute 1 or more cups unbleached
         white flour if desired)

II. *4 teaspoons salt*
     ⅓ cup oil OR butter OR margarine
     3 cups additional whole wheat flour
     1 cup whole wheat flour for kneading

[Makes 2 loaves]

Dissolve the yeast in the water.

Stir in sweetening and dry milk.

Stir in the 4 cups of whole wheat flour to form a thick batter.

Beat well with a spoon (100 strokes).

Let rise 45 minutes.

Fold in the salt and oil.

Fold in an additional 3 cups of flour until the dough comes away from
the sides of the bowl.

Knead on a floured board, using more flour (about 1 cup) as needed to
keep the dough from sticking to the board, about 10 minutes, until the
dough is smooth.

Let rise 50–60 minutes until doubled in size.

Punch down.

Let rise 40–50 minutes until doubled in size.

Shape into loaves and place in pans.

Let rise 20–25 minutes.

Brush tops with Egg Wash (#18).

Bake in a 350° oven for 1 hour, or until golden brown.

Remove from pans and let cool—or eat right away.

Variations: Recipes 2–15 are examples of possible variations of the basic Tassajara Yeasted Bread. All quantities are for two loaves. For each recipe, proceed as with the basic recipe.

Variations include the following:

Water is partially replaced with eggs, sour cream, buttermilk, or mashed banana in some of the recipes.

If you like a lighter bread (and quicker risings), use an additional package of yeast.

The possible sweetenings each have a particular nature and are in some instances specified.

The 4 cups of flour that go into the sponge are specified as "2 cups white and 2 cups whole wheat flour" or "4 cups white flour," and so forth, as the case might be.

For the 3 cups of flour in the second part of the recipe, the following ingredients may be substituted: rye flour, rolled oats, cornmeal, millet meal or whole millet, wheat bran, wheat germ, rice flour, barley flour, soy flour. If cooked grains or cereals are added, additional wheat flour will be necessary to compensate (or the amount of water to start with can be reduced). Generally only one or two of these grains or flours are added in addition to the wheat flour. When more grains are used, the bread tends to lose the distinctiveness of its taste. The use of rice flour, wheat germ, wheat bran, and soy flour in particular will tend to make the bread heavier and denser, although this is also true of any of the flours besides wheat.

Use wheat flour as necessary to knead—more (or less) than 1 cup may be required.

2 Rye–Oatmeal Bread

Darker-colored because of the molasses and rye flour, and flecked with white specks of oats, chewy and moist.

I.   3 cups lukewarm water
     1½ tablespoons dry yeast
     ⅓ cup molasses
     1 cup dry milk
     2 cups unbleached white and 2 cups whole wheat flour

II. 4 teaspoons salt
     ⅓ cup oil
     1½ cups rolled oats
     1½ cups rye flour
     whole wheat flour for kneading

Proceed with the directions in recipe #1.

3 Sesame Bread

This bread has a rich flavor of sesame and a melt-in-the-mouth texture. The sesame meal is so rich with oil that no other oil is needed.

I.   3 cups lukewarm water
     2 packages dry yeast
     ⅓ cup honey
     1 cup dry milk
     2 cups unbleached white and 2 cups whole wheat flour

II. 4 teaspoons salt
     3 cups sesame meal (more if you can stand it)
     2–3 cups whole wheat flour, as necessary to finish forming the
          dough and complete the kneading

Proceed with the directions for recipe #1.

4 White Egg Bread

A good, basic white bread.

I.   *2½ cups lukewarm water*
     2 packages dry yeast
     ¼ cup honey
     1 cup dry milk
     2 eggs, beaten
     4 cups unbleached white flour

II. *4 teaspoons salt*
     ⅓ cup butter or margarine
     3 cups or more unbleached white flour for forming the dough
     1 cup (approx.) white flour for kneading

Proceed with the directions for recipe #1, adding the beaten eggs after stirring in the dry milk.

5 Potato Bread

This white bread is moister and chewier than the white egg bread.

I.   *2 cups warm water*
     2 packages dry yeast
     ¼ cup honey
     1 cup dry milk
     3 cups unbleached white flour

II. *4 teaspoons salt*
     ¼ cup oil
     1½–2 cups cooked mashed potatoes
     3 cups unbleached white flour
     1 cup or more white flour for kneading

Proceed with the directions for recipe #1, folding in the mashed potatoes along with the salt and oil.

6 Summer Swedish Rye Bread

Sweet-smelling and scented, a light bread suitable for sandwiches.

I.   3 cups lukewarm water
     2 packages dry yeast
     ⅓ cup honey
     1 cup dry milk
     grated peel of two oranges
     2 teaspoons anise seeds
     2 teaspoons caraway seeds
     4 cups unbleached white flour

II. 4 teaspoons salt
     ¼ cup oil
     4 cups rye flour
     whole wheat flour for kneading

Proceed with the directions for recipe #1, stirring in the orange peel, anise seeds, and caraway seeds after the dry milk.

7 Cornmeal–Millet Bread

Crunchy, crumbly, and yellow-tinted.

I.   3 cups lukewarm water
     2 packages dry yeast
     ¼ cup honey
     2 cups unbleached white and 2 cups whole wheat flour

II. 4 teaspoons salt
     ¼ cup corn oil
     2½ cups cornmeal
     1½ cups millet meal
     1 cup (approx.) whole wheat flour for forming the dough and
        kneading

Proceed with the directions for recipe #1.

8 Oatmeal Bread

Moist, chewy, and sweet-tasting.

I. 3 cups lukewarm water
    2 packages dry yeast
    1/4 cup honey OR molasses
    1 cup dry milk
    2 cups unbleached white and 2 cups whole wheat flour

II. 4 teaspoons salt
    1/4 cup oil
    2–3 cups rolled oats
    2–3 cups whole wheat flour for forming the dough and kneading

Proceed with the directions for recipe #1.

9 Millet Bread

The millet dots the bread with yellow and provides a flavorful crunchiness.

I. 3 cups whole millet, soaked in 1 1/2 cups very hot tap water
    1 1/2 cups lukewarm water
    2 packages dry yeast
    1/4 cup honey
    1 cup dry milk
    2 cups unbleached white and 2 cups whole wheat flour

II. 4 teaspoons salt
    1/4 cup oil
    soaked millet (see part I)
    3 cups whole wheat flour
    whole wheat flour for kneading

Start the whole millet soaking in the very hot tap water, and then proceed with the directions for recipe #1, folding in the soaked millet after the salt and oil in part II.

10 Banana Sandwich Bread

Fruity, lightly spiced, and especially good for toast and peanut butter sandwiches.

I. *2½ cups lukewarm water*
    2 packages dry yeast
    ¼ cup honey
    1 cup dry milk
    2 bananas, mashed
    2 eggs, beaten
    2 tablespoons cinnamon
    peel of 2 oranges, grated
    2 cups unbleached white flour
    2 or more cups whole wheat flour for forming the sponge

II. *4 teaspoons salt*
    ¼ cup butter OR *margarine*
    3 cups whole wheat flour
    1 cup (approx.) whole wheat flour for kneading

Proceed with the directions for recipe #1, adding the bananas, eggs, cinnamon, and orange peel after the dry milk.

11 Cinnamon Raisin Bread

Nothing to it. Makes excellent toast. Proceed with the directions for recipe # 1, folding in 2 tablespoons cinnamon and 1 cup of raisins along with the salt and oil, using some unbleached white flour if you prefer, in place of whole wheat flour.

12 Nut or Seed Bread

Walnuts? Sunflower seeds? Take your pick. Add a cup or more of any chopped or whole nuts, or seeds of your choosing. These are often better slightly roasted.

13 Fruit Bread

There are a lot of possibilities besides raisins. Add a cup or more of chopped, soaked, or cooked dried fruit: apricot, prune, peach, date, apple.

14 Cheese Bread

Cheese in the bread rather than between the slices makes a flavorful bread for lunch or dinner. It can, of course, also be made into rolls.

I. 3 cups lukewarm water
2 packages dry yeast
1/4 cup brown sugar
1 cup dry milk
2 eggs, beaten
2 cups unbleached white and 2 cups whole wheat flour

II. 2 teaspoons salt
1/2 cup melted butter
3 cups grated Cheddar (or other strong-flavored) cheese
3–5 cups whole wheat flour as required to form the dough and knead it

Proceed with the directions for recipe #1, stirring in the beaten eggs after the dry milk, and folding in the grated cheese after the salt and butter.

15 A French Bread

Crusty, with good wheat flavor. Try a combination of whole wheat and white flour, or use all white flour if you prefer.

I.   *3 cups lukewarm water*
     3 packages dry yeast
     2 tablespoons sugar OR honey
     2 cups unbleached white and 2 cups whole wheat flour

II. *4 teaspoons salt*
     1½ cups unbleached white and 1½ cups whole wheat flour
     wheat flour for kneading

Proceed with the directions for recipe #1. With the additional yeast, rising times will probably be somewhat shorter.

To shape the loaves, follow the instructions in the Sourdough section (page 74) or shape into simple rolls. Place the loaves or rolls on a baking sheet that has been sprinkled with cornmeal. Let them rise for about 20 minutes. Brush with water. Bake at 425° for 10 minutes, and then spray or brush the loaves with water. Continue baking at 375° until well browned—another 15–20 minutes for rolls, another 35–45 minutes for loaves. For added shine and a bit of flavor, brush the tops with garlic butter as soon as the loaves are removed from the oven.

16 Ricotta Olive Bolso

This is a pocket bread with a filling of garlic-herb cheeses, a hearty, ready-made sandwich. The basic filling recipe is followed by optional ingredients to enliven it further, and, of course, you are welcome to dream up more. Mix up the bread dough first, and while it is rising, make up the filling.

If you need help with the bread instructions see "Detailed Instructions," page 15.

Bread for bolso:

    1 package yeast
    1½ cups warm water
    ⅓ cup dry milk
    1 tablespoon honey OR sugar
    2 teaspoons salt

2 tablespoons butter
3¾ cups unbleached white flour OR *whole wheat if preferred*

> [Makes 12 3- by 5-inch bolso
> Preheat oven to 350°]

Dissolve yeast in warm water (about body temperature). Stir in the dry milk, sweetening, salt, and butter. Add a couple of cups of the flour and blend thoroughly, beating until the mixture is elastic. Fold in enough of the remaining flour to make a soft dough, then knead several minutes using more flour as necessary. Let rise 45–60 minutes.

Filling for bolso:

> *1 egg*
> *1 cup grated Cheddar cheese*
> *¾ cup sliced green olives*
> *1 pound ricotta cheese*
> *¾ teaspoon salt (or to taste)*
> *2–3 teaspoons minced fresh oregano* OR *½ teaspoon dried*
> *   oregano*
> *black pepper, freshly ground, to taste*
> *1 or more cloves garlic*

> [Makes filling for 12 bolso]

Beat the egg. Mix in the grated cheese and sliced olives. Blend in the ricotta cheese and then season to taste with the salt, oregano, black pepper, and garlic.

Use 3–4 tablespoons per pocket.

Optional ingredients:
sun-dried tomatoes, slivered
fire-roasted peppers, slivered
Nicoise olives, pitted and chopped
other cheeses: feta, provolone, smoked, some Parmesan or asiago

(Keep in mind that some of the optional cheeses are more salty than the Cheddar in the basic recipe, so you will want to use less salt.)

To make the bolso, divide the dough into 12 pieces and roll each piece into a rectangle or circle. Mound some filling (3–4 tablespoons) on half the dough, then fold over the dough and seal the edges together. Place on a greased baking sheet. Let rise for about 20 minutes, brush the tops with Egg Wash (#18), and bake at 350° for about 45 minutes until golden brown.

These are good hot or cold.

17 Focaccio

Here are some wonderful luncheon (or dinner) rolls: crisp-crusted on the outside, bready on the interior. The olive oil and sage provide a change of flavor.

2 cups lukewarm water
2 packages dry yeast
2 cups whole wheat flour
1 cup unbleached white flour
¼ cup olive oil
2 teaspoons salt
2–3 teaspoons fresh sage or 1 teaspoon dried sage
2 cups whole wheat flour
1 cup or more unbleached white flour

[Makes 8 rolls or baby breads
Preheat oven to 400°]

Mix water and yeast, and then stir in 2 cups of whole wheat and 1 cup of white flour. Beat well and let rise for 30 minutes.

Fold in the olive oil, salt, and sage, and then fold in the second 2 cups of whole wheat flour and as much white flour as necessary to form a soft dough. Knead the dough until it is elastic and smooth, using white flour as necessary.

Divide the dough into 8 pieces, and roll out each piece to a thickness of 1 inch. Put them to rest on oiled baking sheets, and let them rise in a warm place about 25–30 minutes. Bake at 400° for 20 minutes or until slightly golden. Brush with a good olive oil while still hot.

18 Egg Wash

Beat an egg with 2 tablespoons of cold water or milk. Brush on the top of the bread before baking. More water or milk can be used if you want the egg to cover more loaves.

Yeasted Pastries

Yeasted Pastries

The yeasted pastry recipes are generally intended for an occasional, special breakfast treat or perhaps for a picnic. Make one on a leisurely Saturday or Sunday morning, or prepare it the night before, bake to a light brown, and then reheat in the morning to finish the baking to golden brown. These recipes require a little more time, a little more effort, and since the reward is perhaps too tempting, this is quite fortunate.

Traditionally this sort of thing is made entirely with white flour, but whole wheat flour, rolled oats, barley flour, and other flours can be supplemented (as in the variations for the basic Tassajara Yeasted Bread, (#1) for added flavor, chewiness, and grainy sweetness.

Also, as you will see, the various doughs are essentially interchangeable in their possible uses for different shapes and fillings.

19 Yeasted Breakfast Bread Dough

This is like the Tassajara Yeasted Bread (#1), with the addition of eggs and a bit more sweetener and oil. The variations that follow provide ways to make the basic dough into a number of delightful breakfast treats: English muffins, Swedish tea ring, cinnamon rolls, pecan nut rolls, lemon twist bread. See what your feeling dictates and your pantry and waistline allow. This particular dough is not so sweet or rich, but is fairly light; more sweetness comes with the fillings. One loaf makes enough to serve 4–6 people.

I. 1 cup lukewarm water
    3½ teaspoons dry yeast (about 1½ packages)
    3 tablespoons honey OR sugar
    ⅓ cup dry milk
    1 egg
    1½ cups unbleached white OR whole wheat flour

II. 3 tablespoons butter or oil
    1¼ teaspoons salt
    1 cup sifted flour: unbleached white OR whole wheat OR
      your choice
    ½–¾ cup wheat flour for kneading   (continued)

The procedure is the same as for Tassajara Yeasted Bread (#1), except for some different rising times. (You may wish to refer to "Detailed Instructions," page 15.) Here is a review:

Dissolve yeast in water.

Stir in sweetening and dry milk. Stir in egg. (Thorough mixing at this point is not essential.)

Stir in the 1½ cups of wheat flour until a thick batter forms, and then beat well with a spoon (about 100 strokes).

Let rise 30 minutes.

Fold in oil and salt.

Fold in the one cup of flour until the dough comes away from the sides of the bowl.

Knead on a floured board, using more flour (approximately ½–¾ cup, depending on what other flours you used) as needed to keep the dough from sticking to the board and your hands. Knead 5–10 minutes or until the dough is smooth and does not readily tear.

Let rise 40 minutes.

Now the dough is ready to be made into Swedish Tea Ring (#20), Cinnamon Rolls (#22), Pecan Nut Rolls (#23), English Muffins (#24), or Kolaches (#27). Take your pick.

20 Swedish Tea Ring

The dough is rolled up with a fruit filling and then made into a beautiful blossoming flower. (See illustrations.)

For the dough:

> *Yeasted Breakfast Bread Dough (#19)* OR *dough for Norwegian Coffee Cake (#26)* OR *Kolaches (#27)*

For the filling:

1 cup chopped pitted prunes OR *dates* OR *raisins*
½ teaspoon cinnamon (nutmeg or allspice are good too)
1 tablespoon lemon juice OR *orange juice*
¼ cup brown sugar OR *1 teaspoon vanilla extract*
⅛ teaspoon salt

[Preheat oven to 350°]

While the dough is rising, combine the filling ingredients and simmer until thickened.

After the dough has risen, roll it out on a floured board to 12 by 14 inches. Spread with the fruit mixture (Figure 54). Roll as for cinnamon rolls (Figure 55). Place on a greased sheet and join ends (Figure 56). Cut 1-inch slits with scissors (Figure 57), leaving the inner border of the circle intact. Twist as you wish (Figures 58 and 59). (A straight loaf shape may also be made. Leave the roll straight before slitting with the scissors, and then twist the sections to alternate sides.) Allow the loaf to rise to double in bulk (about 20–30 minutes). Brush with Egg Wash (#18). Bake at 350° for 30–40 minutes until golden brown. Be aware that if the loaf is as pictured in Figure 59, the sections in the middle will take longer to bake than those on the outside. Frost with Powdered Sugar Glaze (recipe 21) if you wish.

2 I Powdered Sugar Glaze

Here is the simplest way to make a glaze for topping your breakfast pastries. This recipe makes enough for one batch of the accompanying recipes. If you want a lot of glaze, double it.

1 cup sifted powdered sugar
4–6 teaspoons milk OR *cream* OR *lemon juice*

Sift the powdered sugar and mix in the liquid. (Add more liquid if you want to make it thinner.) The glaze may be flavored with vanilla extract or the zested peel of a lemon or an orange.

Frost the pastry when it is hot from the oven.

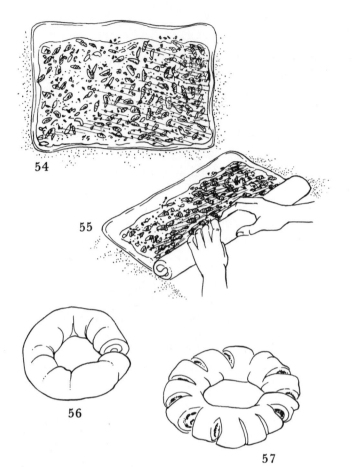

54

55

56

57

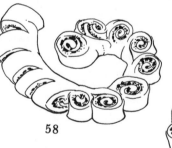

58

59

22 Cinnamon Rolls

What a revelation it was making cinnamon rolls for the first time! They are still one of my favorites.

For the dough:

> *Yeasted Breakfast Bread Dough (#19)* OR *dough for Norwegian Coffee Cake (#26)* OR *Kolaches (#27)*

For the filling:

> *¼ cup softened or melted butter*
> *¾ cup brown sugar*
> *1 tablespoon or more cinnamon*
> *½ cup or more raisins*

[Preheat oven to 375°]

Prepare the dough. After it has risen, roll it out on a floured board in a rectangle ¼–⅜ inch thick. Spread on the softened butter or brush on the melted butter.

Sprinkle on the brown sugar, cinnamon, and raisins. (These quantities make a fairly sweet cinnamon roll, but you can use more or less of these ingredients as you prefer.)

Starting at one edge, roll up the dough fairly tight as you would a carpet. (See Figure 55, which shows this same procedure for the Swedish Tea Ring.) Cut the roll in sections about ½–¾ inch thick, and place the sections flat on a greased baking sheet, leaving space around them to rise and spread out. Let them rise for 20 minutes.

Brush with Egg Wash (#18) and bake at 375° for about 20–25 minutes, until golden brown.

Frost with Powdered Sugar Glaze (#21).

23 Pecan Nut Rolls

Baked on a bed of sugar, butter, and nuts, the pecan nut rolls are turned upside down out of the pan so that they have a sweet, syrupy topping. Since the rolls are nestled in the pan next to each other, they rise up and not out, and make a tender and light roll with little crust.

For the dough:

> *Yeasted Breakfast Bread Dough (#19)* OR *dough for Norwegian Coffee Cake (#26)* OR *Kolaches (#27)*

For the filling:

> *¼ cup softened or melted butter*
> *¾ cup or less brown sugar*
> *1 tablespoon or more cinnamon*
> *½ cup or more raisins*
> *1 cup or more chopped pecans (or walnuts or other nuts)*
>
> *6 tablespoons butter*
> *½ cup brown sugar*

[Serves 4–6]

Prepare the nut rolls according to the directions for Cinnamon Rolls (#22), adding ½ cup or more of chopped pecans along with the raisins. (You may want to use less sugar in the filling.) Use two cake pans or two pans 8 inches square. Dot the bottom of *each* pan with 3 tablespoons butter and ¼ cup brown sugar, along with an additional ¼ cup or more of chopped pecans. Place the cut rolls next to each other on top of this mixture. Let rise for 20–30 minutes and bake at 350° for 30 minutes until golden brown. Turn upside down onto a serving platter.

24 English Muffins

These favorites can be made with any yeasted bread dough. They keep well, refrigerated or frozen.

> *Yeasted Breakfast Bread Dough (#19) or another yeasted bread dough*

Make up a batch of Yeasted Breakfast Bread Dough. Or make a dough from recipes #1–15 (with or without the addition of eggs). One-third to one-half a batch will make the same number of muffins as the Yeasted Breakfast Bread Dough. (The rest of the batch can still be made into a loaf of bread.)

After the dough has risen, punch it down and let it rest for 10 minutes. Roll out the dough on a floured board about ¼ to ⅜ inch thick and cut into 3-inch rounds or squares. Sprinkle the tops with cornmeal.

Cover with a dry towel and let muffins rise on the board until doubled in size (30–45 minutes).

Bake slowly on an ungreased griddle. For each side start the griddle hot, and then reduce heat to brown slowly, cooking 5–8 minutes on each side.

If the middles of the muffins still seem doughy, put them in a 350° oven for a few minutes to finish baking.

25 Lemon Twist Bread

The tangy lemon scent of this bread freshens the morning air.

> *Yeasted Breakfast Bread Dough (#19)*
> *½ cup raisins*
> *1 tablespoon grated lemon peel*
> *1 teaspoon freshly grated nutmeg*

Follow the Yeasted Breakfast Bread Dough recipe, adding the raisins, lemon peel, and nutmeg to the sponge.

After the dough has risen once, punch it down and let it rise again. Then divide into as many pieces as you would like to braid, roll out each piece into a strand, and braid. (Illustration for braiding four or six strands are on pages 56–57.)

Place the loaf on a greased cookie sheet and let it rise for 20–30 minutes until doubled. Brush with Egg Wash (#18).

Bake at 350° for 40 minutes or until golden brown. Frost with Powdered Sugar Glaze (#21), using lemon juice and grated lemon peel.

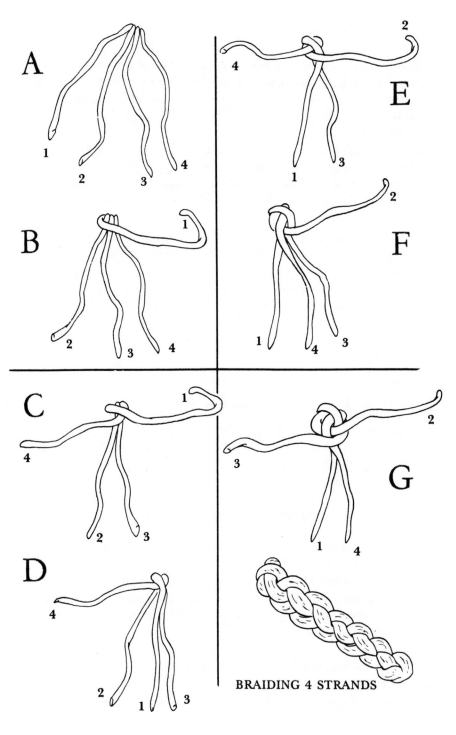

BRAIDING 4 STRANDS

56

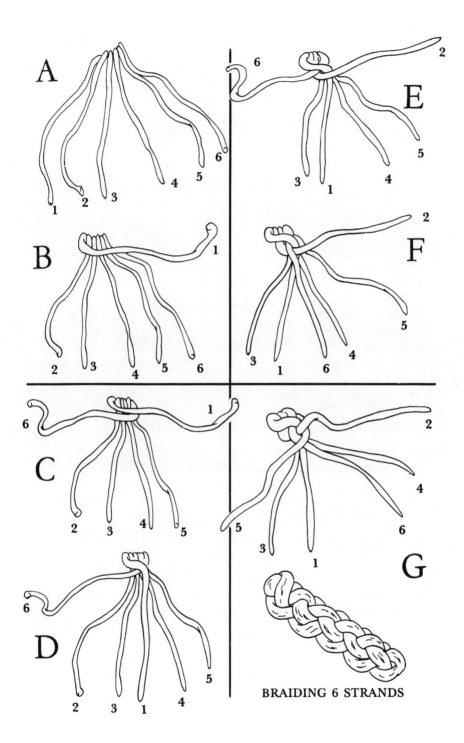

A

B

C

D

E

F

G

BRAIDING 6 STRANDS

26 Norwegian Coffee Cake

Rich with butter, sugar, and eggs, this dough can be made into a large braided loaf, or used for Cinnamon Rolls, Pecan Nut Rolls, or Kolaches. The recipe makes a larger amount of dough than the Yeasted Breakfast Bread Dough, so you might be prepared to do some of each.

2 packages dry yeast (about 1½ tablespoons)
1¼ cups lukewarm water OR milk (if using whole milk, scald and
  cool to lukewarm)
1½ cups unbleached white flour
⅝ cup brown sugar
½ cup butter OR margarine
3 eggs
1 teaspoon salt
½ teaspoon freshly ground cardamom
lemon or orange peel (optional)
½ cup raisins (optional)
3–3½ cups white or whole wheat flour, as needed

[Serves 6–8]

Dissolve yeast in liquid and stir in the 1½ cups of white flour, adding a couple of tablespoons of the sugar. Beat well, and set aside to rise.

Cream the butter or margarine, and then cream in the sugar.

Beat in the eggs, one at a time.

Fold the butter mixture into the yeast sponge along with the salt and cardamom. Then fold in flour (3–3½ cups) as necessary to form a soft dough. Knead the dough until smooth, using more flour as needed.

Let the dough rise until doubled in size (30–40 minutes).

Pick a shape. Place in or on a greased pan. Let loaf rise to double, about 20–30 minutes.

Apply Egg Wash (#18) and bake at 350°–375° for about 45–50 minutes or until golden brown.

Frost with Powdered Sugar Glaze (#21).

27 Kolaches

Kolaches are little Czech pastries with a sweet filling. Recipes for possible fillings follow the recipe for the dough. These are fun for breakfast, picnics, or parties.

2 packages dry yeast (about 1½ tablespoons)
1¼ cups lukewarm water OR milk, scalded and cooled
1½ cups sifted unbleached white flour
½ cup brown sugar OR honey
⅜ cup butter OR margarine
2 eggs
1 teaspoon salt
¼ teaspoon anise extract OR ½ teaspoon ground anise seed
½ teaspoon mace OR nutmeg
3 cups (more or less) unbleached white or whole wheat flour

[Makes approx. 24 pastries]

Soften yeast in liquid. Stir in the unbleached white flour and a little of the sugar. Beat well, about 100 times, cover, and set aside to rise.

Cream the butter with the sugar or honey, and then beat in the eggs, one at a time.

Fold the butter mixture into the risen yeast sponge, along with the salt and spices. Fold in additional wheat flour as necessary to form a soft dough. Knead for several minutes, adding more flour as needed to form a soft, smooth dough.

Let rise until doubled in volume. Punch down, divide into individual pieces (walnut to egg size), shape into balls, and place on greased cookie sheets, leaving room to rise and spread. Flatten to ½-inch height and let rise for 20 minutes.

Make an indentation in each pastry with your thumb and put the filling in it. Let them rise 10 minutes, brush with egg wash or melted butter.

Bake at 350° for 20 minutes, or until golden brown.

Another method to make Kolaches: After the first rising, roll the dough out to a thickness of ¼ inch, and cut into squares. Place a spoonful of filling in the center of each square, then twist the opposite corners together over the filling. Pinch the corners tightly together or they will come apart. Let them rise for 10–15 minutes, apply Egg Wash (#18), and bake as above.

KOLACHE TOPPINGS AND FILLINGS

Poppy Seed Topping

> 2 cups ground poppy seed
> 1 cup brown or raw sugar
> 1/2 cup honey
> 1 1/2 cups milk
> 1/2 teaspoon salt

Mix well, and cook slowly for 20 minutes until thick yet spreadable. Cool before putting on dough.

Butter Glaze

> 1 cup brown or raw sugar
> 1/2 cup unbleached white flour, sifted
> 1/3 cup butter

Cut butter into sugar and flour, and place on top of poppy seed, prune, or apricot fillings just before placing Kolaches in oven.

Prune or Apricot Filling

> 2 cups cooked, mashed, pitted prunes or apricots
> 1/2 cup honey
> 1 tablespoon lemon juice

Mix until ingredients are well blended.
Also try cherry, apple, pineapple, peach, or berry filling for Kolaches.

Almond Paste

> 2 eggs, well beaten
> 1/2 pound ground almonds
> honey to taste

Mix eggs and almonds, and add honey to taste.

Date Almond Filling

¼ cup butter
¼ cup honey
¾ cup whole pitted dates
¼ cup almond paste OR chopped almonds

Melt butter and sugar together, stir in remaining ingredients, and cook until thickened.

28 Braided Christmas Bread

Grandmother must have made this bread every Christmas for sixty or seventy years. Married in 1903, she raised four daughters and a son. She lost her husband and lived long enough to see all her children die except for one daughter—and went on baking bread.

In her room the white paint on the ceiling and walls was peeling, revealing the blue underneath, like clouds in the heavens. In a huge vase were a multitude of flowers, fresh and plastic mixed. All around were the fruits of her handiwork: rag rugs made from whatever scraps were available, embroidered tablecloths and dresser runners, crocheted hot-plate covers, patchwork quilts.

Although she came to this country at the age of eighteen, even late in life she spoke little English. We spent our time together laughing and giggling—and baking bread. Of course we didn't measure anything, except by hand or eye or feel.

¼ cup lukewarm water
3 packages dry yeast
½ cup sugar OR honey
2 cups milk, scalded
¼ cup butter OR margarine
3½ cups unbleached white flour
3 eggs
1½ tablespoons salt
½ teaspoon mace
1 teaspoon vanilla extract
½ cup raisins
½ cup chopped walnuts OR pecans OR almonds
½–1 cup candied fruit peel OR citron OR cherries (optional)
4 cups wheat flour (with variations as in Tassajara Yeasted Bread)
(continued)

[1 very large loaf or several smaller ones]

Dissolve the yeast in the lukewarm water with a little sugar added. Combine the remaining sugar with the milk and butter. When this mixture is cool enough (body temperature), add the yeast mixture.

Add the 3½ cups of white flour to make a soft sponge, stirring well with a wooden spoon. Set aside to rise.

While the dough is rising, separate the eggs, and beat the yolks and whites separately. Fold the yolks into the sponge and then the whites. Let it rise until doubled in bulk, about 40 minutes.

Fold in the salt, mace, vanilla, raisins, nuts, and optional candied fruit. Fold in more wheat flour until a dough is formed, and knead on a floured board, adding more flour as necessary. Knead well (125–150 times).

Place in a buttered bowl and let rise until doubled in size—about 50 minutes.

Place the dough on a floured board. Work it into a ball or cylinder and divide into nine equal pieces. Roll each piece into a length of 14 inches. Pinch four lengths together at one end and intertwine them (see illustration showing the braiding of four strands, page 56). Place this on a well-greased cookie sheet to provide the bottom layer of the loaf. Then braid three lengths and place them on top of the bottom layer. Finally twist together two lengths and place them on top of the second layer. Press the braided lengths together well, since they tend to topple over. Straighten before baking, and perhaps while baking.

Now beat up an extra egg, add a little coolish water, and brush the top of the braids all over. Let rise for about 20 minutes, while the oven is preheating to 300°.

Bake for an hour or a little longer until well browned.

Happy Holidays!

Unyeasted Breads

Unyeasted Breads

This section has been greatly reduced from the original edition. I have kept what I consider to be the best examples of the sort of breads that can be done without yeast or other rising agents.

Unyeasted breads have a deep, hearty, honest spirit with a certain substantial integrity. Dense and thick-crusted, they require a good bread knife for cutting and a certain endurance for chewing. However, some (such as Overnight Unyeasted Bread) can be made surprisingly light.

No matter how much I mentioned the dense, "bricklike" nature of some of these breads, still I received many letters from people wondering why the bread came out of the oven like a piece of building material. O.K., they are not to everyone's taste, but some people really like this sort of thing: "How real," they say, "How flavorful."

Now for some pointers. Warm or boiling water is used because it makes a softer dough that is easier to handle. Make the dough slightly moist before kneading, as more flour can be incorporated during the kneading. Keep enough flour on the board so that the dough does not stick, and scrape up any dough that sticks and reincorporate it into the mass of dough.

Follow the instruction for kneading given on page 20. When the kneading is first begun, the dough will tear rather than stretch, but keep working with it until it is smooth and elastic (about 300 kneads). Resting now and again is permitted.

Make the dough into loaves following the directions given for yeasted bread (page 26).

When the loaves are in the pans, make a wedge-shaped slit the length of each loaf with a knife.

Brush the tops of the loaves with warm water or oil to keep them moist while they sit before baking.

The baking times and temperatures are different for different recipes. You may discover some times and temperatures that you prefer. So much the better.

But remember, if you want a nice, light bread, turn to the Yeasted Breads section.

29 Tibetan Barley Bread

Many people find this to be one of the best unyeasted breads. But remember, it is dense and thick-crusted. Consider it a relic from the sixties. Does anyone still eat this way?

2 cups barley flour
2 tablespoons sesame oil
4 cups whole wheat flour
½ cup millet meal OR *roasted sunflower* OR *sesame seeds*
1½ teaspoons salt
2 tablespoons corn oil
3½ cups boiling water

[Makes 1 large loaf]

Pan-roast the barley flour in the sesame oil until darkened.

Mix it together with the flour, meal, and salt.

Add the corn oil, rubbing the flour between your hands until it becomes oily.

Add the boiling water a little at a time, mixing with a spoon until a dough begins to form, then mixing with your hands. Keep your hands cool by dipping them in a bowl of cold water. Mix the dough until it has an earlobe consistency, and then knead it until smooth.

Place the dough in an oiled pan. Cut the top lengthwise, making a deep wedge in the loaf. Proof 2–6 hours or overnight.

Bake at 450° for 20 minutes on the middle shelf, then 400° on the top shelf. The crust will be tough but the inside tender. You can also try baking at 350° for 1½ hours.

30 Overnight Unyeasted Bread I

A bread with primitive intensity. It has a deliciously wheaty taste and is remarkably high-rising considering that it has no yeast, unsweetened, with thick crusts and softish interior.

7 cups whole wheat flour
1 tablespoon salt
warm water as needed, about 3½ cups

Combine the salt with the flour, and add water, mixing with a spoon, until a dough begins to form. Knead 300 times (count them), cover with a wet towel, and let sit 12–24 hours in a warm place.

Knead 100 times, shape into a loaf, and place in an oiled pan. Cut the top lengthwise and let proof for 4 hours in a warm place, or 1½–2 hours in a 100°–120° oven.

Bake at 350° for 30 minutes, then at 400° for 45–60 minutes. The crust will be dark brown.

If you like this sort of bread, you can of course experiment with the use of other flours in addition to the whole wheat, using a minimum of 4 cups of whole wheat to start with. You could also add ¼ cup of oil per loaf and even a little yeast.

3 I Overnight Unyeasted Bread II

This recipe demonstrates how to make a simple bread using leftover oatmeal and brown rice.

3 cups whole wheat flour
3 cups unbleached white flour
1 tablespoon salt
2–3 cups leftover cereals (oatmeal and brown rice or others)
warm water as needed

[Makes 1 large loaf]

Mix the flours together with the salt and work in the leftover cereals. If the mixture is too dry to form a dough, add warm water a little at a time until the dough is of kneading consistency. (Since the cooked cereals supply moisture, chances are that not much water will be needed.) On the other hand, if the mixture is too wet after adding the cereals, add more flour to form a dough.

Knead well (300 times), place in a bowl, cover with a wet towel, and let sit 12–16 hours in a warm place.

Knead 100 times, shape into a loaf, and place in an oiled pan. Slit the top deeply, and let rise for 2 hours in a briefly heated oven (350° for 5 minutes).

Bake at 375° for 30 minutes, then at 450° for 30–45 minutes. The sides of the loaf will be very dark brown.

32 Unyeasted Dutch Rye Bread

This is the kind of pumpernickel rye with a texture reminiscent of salami. Though dense and heavy, the loaf can be thin-sliced to provide a soft-chewing and flavorful accompaniment to cheeses and cold cuts.

> 4 cups rye meal (coarsely cracked rye that contains some flour)
> 1 cup cracked wheat
> 1½ teaspoons salt
> 2 tablespoons honey OR molasses
> 2 tablespoons oil
> ¼ cup wheat bran
> 3–3¼ cups boiling water
>
> wheat germ

[Makes 1 large loaf]

Mix all the ingredients together to form a wet dough. Cover and let sit overnight.

Add more bran or wheat flour if necessary in order to shape a loaf. Roll the loaf in bran or wheat germ to coat.

Bake in a covered pan for 4 hours at 200° with a pan of hot water on a lower shelf. (Refill the pan with water as necessary.)

After removing the loaf from the oven, let it cool completely, then wrap it in a moist towel and refrigerate it for one or two days before serving. Slice thin.

33 Gruel Bread

Here is an unusual way to turn leftovers into the "staff of life." Once a "most popular" bread at Tassajara, we still make it on rare occasions. The bread has a texture similar to sourdough: coarse, but fairly light with a thick crust.

> 4 cups rice gruel (cooked-together leftover rice or other grains,
>   soups, vegetables)
> 1 teaspoon salt OR soy sauce
> ¼ cup oil (optional)
> 6 cups whole wheat flour (amount will vary according to how
>   moist the gruel is)

Mix the salt and oil into the gruel, and add flour ½ cup or so at a time. Mix by stirring and then by hand until a dough forms with earlobe consistency, firm yet pliable. Knead on a floured board until smooth, about 300 times.

Make into a loaf and place in an oiled bread pan. Brush the top with water and make a ½-inch-deep cut down the center of the loaf. Cover with a damp towel, and set in a warm place overnight.

Bake at 350°–375° for 75–90 minutes, until the sides and bottom are dark brown.

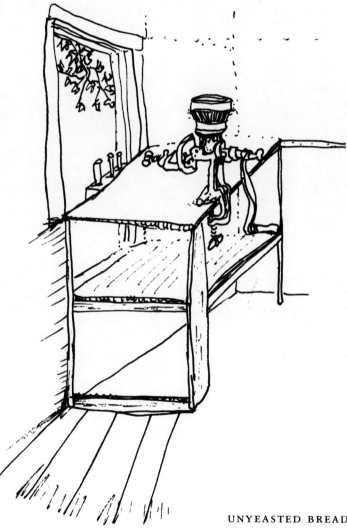

Sourdough Breads
& Pancakes

Sourdough Breads & Pancakes

It is surely a wonder of nature that something sour or "spoiled" can make bread rise and delicious besides. Sourdough is probably the easiest bread to make (once you have a good starter), and its flavor is exquisitely distinctive and exciting. I have included in this section sourdough French, sourdough rye, and sourdough pancakes.

A starter is required in the making of sourdough bread. Growing in the starter are microorganisms that cause the bread to rise and give it its characteristic sour taste. The starter is mixed with flour and water to form a sponge (similar to the sponge for yeasted bread), which then sits overnight. By morning the entire mixture is sour. Some of the sponge is removed to replenish the starter before other ingredients are added. To replenish the starter, fill a jar or crock (not metal) only half full, as the starter will rise some as it sits. Cover and keep refrigerated.

A sourdough starter can be made by combining 1 tablespoon of dry yeast, 2½ cups warm water, 2 teaspoons sugar or honey, and 2½ cups flour. Cover and let it ferment for five days, stirring daily. The starter may be kept indefinitely in the refrigerator, although it is probably best to use it once a week or so. If liquid rises to the top during storage, stir it in again. The starter and the sponge are both the consistency of thick mud.

Another way to make a sourdough starter is to take any sour food, such as two-day-old or older rice, cereal, coconut, fruit, vegetables, or milk, and mix it with 2½ cups whole wheat flour and enough water to make the dough spongy. Cover and let it sit for 3–4 days, stirring daily, until a distinctly sour smell arises.

34 Sourdough Bread

Here is a basic recipe for sourdough bread. The dough can also be made into English Muffins (recipe #24).

At night:

> 5 cups whole wheat flour
> 1–1½ cups starter
> 4 cups lukewarm water

(continued)

In the morning:

Replenish the starter.
½ cup oil
1 tablespoon salt
5–6 cups or more whole wheat flour

[Makes 2 loaves]

At night, add the starter to 5 cups of flour without mixing. Then mix together while adding water gradually, until a thick, pasty batter is formed. Beat well. Cover and set aside overnight.

In the morning, remove 1–1½ cups from the sponge to replenish the starter, and refrigerate it for the next batch. Now fold into the sponge the oil, salt, and remaining flour gradually with a spoon. When the dough comes away from the sides of the bowl, remove to a floured bread board. Knead for 5 minutes, adding more flour as necessary. The dough will be a little softer and stickier than normal yeasted bread.

Cut into two pieces and form into loaves. To make French loaves, see recipe #36. The loaves can also be shaped into balls (and baked on a sheet) or standard loaves (and baked in oiled bread pans). Slit the tops with lengthwise gashes. Allow 2 hours for rising.

Brush or spritz the tops with water and place in a preheated 425° oven for 20 minutes. Brush or spritz the tops with water again, turn the oven down to 375°, and continue baking for an hour or so until the loaves are nicely browned.

35 Sourdough Rye Bread

A simple variation on the basic sourdough bread provides the delicatessen taste.

Substitute 3–4 cups of rye flour for the whole wheat flour in the morning addition. Shape into round loaves and bake on a greased sheet or on a baking sheet sprinkled with cornmeal. Bake as in the basic recipe (#34).

36 Sourdough French Loaves

Here is one procedure for shaping French loaves. Using unbleached white flour in place of some or all of the whole wheat in the Sourdough Bread recipe will produce a more traditional loaf.

To shape the French loaves, roll the dough out in a rectangle about ¼ inch thick on a floured board. Then roll up the dough tightly, as you would roll up a carpet.

Pinch the seam together and roll the loaf about to shape it evenly. Place the finished loaf, seam down, on a baking sheet that has been sprinkled with cornmeal. Brush the loaves with water. Make a ½-inch-deep lengthwise slit in the top.

Let rise and bake as for the regular Sourdough Bread loaves (#34).

37 Sourdough Pancakes

Heavenly.

At night:

> *Mix up sourdough sponge as for sourdough bread (2½ cups whole wheat flour to 2 cups water with ½ cup starter).*

In the morning:

> *Replenish your starter store from this new batch. For every 2½ cups of whole wheat flour used in original sponge, add:*
> *1 egg, beaten*
> *2 tablespoons corn oil*
> *¾–1 cup milk*
> *1 teaspoon salt*
> *1 teaspoon baking soda*
> *2 tablespoons brown sugar*

[Serves 2–6]

Mix dough thoroughly with egg, oil, and milk. Combine salt, soda, and brown sugar, and sprinkle over batter. Fold in gently. Let sit a few minutes before frying. Small pancakes seem to cook better.

Variations: Add fresh chopped fruit to batter: apples, bananas, peaches, plums, nectarines, apricots.

Add chopped nuts or seeds to batter: sunflower, pine, chopped walnuts, chopped almond, toasted sesame seeds.

Add spices as desired: cinnamon, nutmeg, mace, or coriander.

38 Country French Bread

This is about as bread as you can get: flour, salt, water, yeast, and sour-dough starter. A wonderfully coarse and bready texture with intense wheat flavor, this bread is basically a sourdough, but with a little yeast boost—one of our perennial favorites.

At night:

>   1−1½ cups sourdough starter
>   5 cups whole wheat flour
>   3½ cups warm water

In the morning:

>   Replenish the starter.
>   1 teaspoon dry yeast
>   ¼ cup water
>   1 tablespoon salt
>   4−6 cups unbleached white flour

[Makes 2 moderate loaves]

At night, add the starter to the flour, then mix in the water a little at a time until it is all added. Beat well. Cover and set aside overnight. A warm but not hot place is preferable but not essential.

In the morning, replenish the starter and refrigerate it for the next batch of sourdough bread. Dissolve the yeast in the water and let it sit for 5 minutes. Then stir it into the sponge along with the salt.

Fold in the white flour a cup at a time until a dough forms. Remove from the bowl to a floured board and knead thoroughly, adding more flour as necessary.

Divide the dough into two pieces, shape each piece into a ball, and place on an oiled baking sheet. Let the loaves rise until about doubled in size (1½−2 hours).

Make a few slits in the tops, brush or spritz them with water, and place the loaves in a 425° oven for 20 minutes. Brush the tops with water again, turn the oven down to 375°, and continue baking for 50−60 minutes or until well browned.

39 Sourdough Raisin Rolls

These rolls made by our bakery are unique and unusual—a sourdough sweetened with raisins and cinnamon. Although the rolls are simple to make, some prior preparation is necessary. We keep a sourdough starter just for the raisin rolls, and in addition to this starter a batch of fermented raisins is needed. The raisins take several days to ferment, and the rolls themselves take nearly a day, so plan ahead!

1 teaspoon salt
1 teaspoon cinnamon
4 cups whole wheat flour
1 cup sourdough raisin roll starter (could be your usual sourdough
    starter for the first batch of rolls)
1¾ cups raisin water
½ cup fermented raisins
⅔ cup raisins
whole wheat flour as needed

[Makes 12 large or more smaller rolls]

Note: The sourdough raisin roll starter ends up containing raisins, fermented raisins, and raisin water, unlike the plain sourdough starter. But of course a plain starter can be used for the first batch of raisin rolls.

Mix the salt and cinnamon with the flour. Put the starter on top of the flour, and stir in the raisin water (see below) a little at a time to form a soft dough. When the mixture is too thick to stir, work with your hands. Knead for several minutes and then knead in the fermented raisins (see below) and the dry raisins. Keep the dough on the moist side as much as possible, but add more flour as needed to keep it from being too sticky to work with. Let the dough sit for 20 minutes or so, and then replenish the starter.

Divide the dough into twelve pieces for large rolls or more pieces for smaller rolls. Shape into balls and place them on an oiled baking sheet. Cover with a damp towel and let them sit overnight (15 hours or more).

Bake at 375° for 20–25 minutes or until well browned. (Smaller rolls will bake more quickly.)

Fermented Raisins and Raisin Water: Place ½ cup of raisins in 2 cups of water. Cover and let sit for 3–4 days, unrefrigerated. Stir daily. If you are making sourdough raisin rolls regularly, you can keep a continuous batch of raisins going. We use all the water and a portion of the raisins each day, and then replenish both.

Pancakes & Other Things to Eat for Breakfast, Lunch, or Dinner

Pancakes & Other Things to Eat for Breakfast, Lunch, or Dinner

Pancakes are real heartwarmers, especially for Zen students who have been breakfasting on cereal, beans, and fruit or pickled vegetables. Oftentimes a first stop on the way out of Tassajara is for pancakes with plenty of syrup. More impatient students, sleepless with desire, have been known to sneak into the still-of-night kitchen and fry up a few of their favorites (with all sorts of optional ingredients in the batter or on top of the finished pancake: honey, tahini, peanut butter, blueberries, bananas, roasted nuts or seeds). Generous souls when satiated, they usually tidy up after themselves and leave a couple of pancakes for the kitchen crew.

No special tricks are involved in making pancakes. Heat a frying pan or griddle until sprinkled-on water dances around briefly before evaporating. Fry the pancakes on the first side until small bubbles appear in the uncooked surface. Turn (once only) and fry the other side. If the center is not cooking or if browning is spotty or uneven, the pan is too hot.

The other recipes in this section—popovers, cream scones, biscuits, and bagels—also can make a heartwarming offering any time of the day or night. Coffee cake? As you like it.

40 Whole Wheat Pancakes

To have originally called these pancakes "entirely exceptional" sounds extravagant after all these years, but they certainly are good, especially served with jam-marbled sour cream or butter and maple syrup.

> 2 cups whole wheat pastry flour
> 3 teaspoons baking powder
> 1 teaspoon salt
> 1 tablespoon brown sugar OR honey
> 2 cups milk
> ½ cup oil OR melted butter
> 3 egg yolks, beaten
> 3 egg whites, stiffly beaten

(continued)

Sift the flour with the baking powder, salt, and sugar. If using honey, add it to the milk and oil. Beat the milk and oil into the beaten yolks.

Combine the milk mixture with the dry ingredients until just blended, and then fold in the stiffly beaten egg whites.

Cook on a greased griddle or frying pan. May be made any size—the larger ones will take longer to cook through.

Variations: May be made with fruit purée (apple, apricot, peach, pear) in place of the milk.

Fruit chunks may be folded into the batter. Blueberries, bananas, and apple are particularly good.

Nut butters may be added to the wet ingredients.

Roasted nuts or sesame or sunflower seeds may be folded into the batter.

Cornmeal, rolled oats, barley flour, or buckwheat flour (½ cup) may be substituted in place of an equivalent amount of whole wheat flour.

For waffles, use only 1¼ cups of milk.

4I Orange Whole Wheat Hotcakes

These are fragrant, but you may still prefer your orange juice on the side.

> 2 eggs, beaten
> ¼ cup oil
> 2 cups sifted whole wheat flour
> ½ teaspoon baking soda
> ½ teaspoon salt
> 2 cups freshly squeezed orange juice

[Serves 2–6]

Mix eggs and oil, and beat. Combine dry ingredients and add to the egg mixture alternately with the orange juice.

Blend well. Griddle.

42 O-Konomi-Yaki

Japanese pancakes made with vegetables (and meat) can be served as a midnight meal with warm results. Americans put butter on everything (or used to); Japanese prefer soy sauce, but syrup, no.

¼ Chinese, green, or red cabbage
1 carrot
½ onion
2 celery stalks
½ cup meat or fish pieces (optional)
2 cups (or more) whole wheat or unbleached white flour, or both
1 egg, beaten
2 tablespoons brown sugar
1 teaspoon salt
1 tall can evaporated milk
enough water to make batter

[Serves 5–6]

Chop, shred, dice, or thinly slice vegetables (and meat). It is essential that the pieces be small so that the pancakes are not too thick. Mix together the remaining ingredients to form a batter. Fold in the vegetables and proceed to grill. If the pancakes are not cooking in the middle, thin the batter some and cook more slowly. These may also be eaten cold on a picnic.

43 Cottage Cheese Pancakes

Creamy and blintz-rich without a filling.

6 eggs
6 tablespoons whole wheat or unbleached white flour
¼ teaspoon salt
2 cups cottage cheese

[Makes 24 small to medium pancakes]

Separate the eggs, beat the whites stiff, and set aside. Beat the yolks and then beat in the flour, salt, and cottage cheese. Fold in the egg whites. Grill, or fry in buttered pan.

44 Popovers

Puffy and eggy buns with space for stuffing.

> 1 cup unbleached white flour
> ½ teaspoon salt
> 3 eggs, beaten
> 1 cup milk
> 2 tablespoons melted butter

[Makes 12 popovers
Preheat oven to 450°]

Use a popover pan or regular muffin tins. Mix ingredients thoroughly. Grease the muffin tins and heat in the oven for 5–10 minutes. When hot, fill each cup one-third full with popover batter. Bake at 450° for 20 minutes, then reduce the heat to 350° and bake another 10–20 minutes. Do not open the oven until after 30 minutes of baking or the popovers may fall.

Serve with butter, jam, or cheese. Or serve for dinner stuffed with meat or vegetables in cream or cheese sauce; with grains, vegetables, or stuffing; or with a mushroom filling. Heck, or just plain buttered.

45 Apple Pancake Sam

Here is a giant, clove-scented popover with apples that makes a quick but memorable breakfast dish.

> 2 tablespoons butter
> juice of 1 lemon
> 1 medium apple, sliced into wedges
> 2 tablespoons brown sugar
> ½ cup flour
> ½ cup milk
> 3 eggs
> ground cloves

[Serves 2
Preheat oven to 400°]

Put the butter into an 8- or 9-inch round baking dish and heat in the oven at 400° for 10 minutes. Do not brown.

Meanwhile, squeeze the lemon juice over the apple slices and toss with the brown sugar.

In a mixing bowl, combine the flour, milk, and eggs. Whisk briefly until barely together. Batter will be lumpy. Remove the baking dish from the oven and pour in the batter. Arrange the apples in a circle around the dish, putting 2 or 3 in the center. Top with the remaining lemon juice—brown sugar mixture.

Bake for 25 minutes until firm and puffy. Dust with a sprinkling of ground cloves and serve with warmed pure maple syrup.

In the summer use fresh blueberries in place of the apples.

To serve 4, this recipe may be doubled and baked in a 15- to 16-inch dish.

46 Cream Scones

A guest-season favorite, these scones have a soft, velvety texture and a tangy taste.

• Bake at 400° for 24 mins, in slices
• 23 minutes as cake, then slice

1 cup sour milk OR buttermilk
6 tablespoons sugar OR honey ½c,
1 egg
3½ cups unbleached white or half whole wheat flour
2 heaping teaspoons cream of tartar
1 heaping teaspoon baking soda
½ cup melted butter OR oil

[Serves 4–6]

Note: Raw milk will sour much better than pasteurized.

Blend together the sour milk, sugar, and egg. Sift in the flour with the cream of tartar and soda. Beat well and gradually add the melted butter. Keep the dough moist.

Add up to ½ cup more flour as necessary to roll out. Roll out ¼–⅜ inch thick, cut into triangular wedges, and dust with flour. Bake slowly on a griddle or in a frying pan over medium low heat so that the center will bake (5–7 minutes a side). These can also be baked in the oven.

Variation: Add ¼–½ cup currants or raisins.

47 Flaky Biscuits

Tender, flaky, grandly high-rising, this recipe is adaptable to a number of variations listed below and also can be used as a quick dough for cinnamon rolls.

> 1 cup unbleached white flour
> 1 cup whole wheat flour
> 3 teaspoons baking powder
> ½ teaspoon salt
> ½ cup butter OR margarine
> 2 eggs
> ½ cup milk

[Makes 12–16 biscuits
Preheat oven to 450°]

Combine flours, baking powder, and salt. Cut butter or margarine into dry ingredients with a pastry cutter or two knives, or rub gently between hands until pea-sized pieces are formed. Make a well in the center and add the eggs and milk. Beat the eggs and milk with a fork until smoothish. Then continue stirring with the fork, gradually incorporating flour, until all is moistened. On a floured board, knead the dough just enough to bring it together.

Roll the dough into a rectangle ½ inch thick. Fold in thirds. Turn the dough a quarter turn, and repeat rolling and folding. Repeat once more. (The rolling and folding make a flakier biscuit.)

To make the biscuits, roll out the dough again to a ½-inch thickness. Cut into rounds with a floured cutter or glass. Place on an ungreased sheet, and bake at 450° for 8–10 minutes until the bottoms are browned lightly and the tops slightly golden. Keep an eye on them— they get dry if overbaked.

For sesame seed or sunflower seed biscuits:
Add ½ cup roasted sesame or sunflower seeds with the dry ingredients.

48 Basil and Parmesan Cheese Flaky Biscuits

A flavorful biscuit variation well suited to lunch or dinner.

ingredients for Flaky Biscuits (#47)
1¾ cups grated Parmesan cheese
2 tablespoons minced fresh basil leaves

[Makes 12–16 biscuits]

Follow the directions for Flaky Biscuits, stirring the grated cheese and minced basil leaves into the flour–butter mixture before adding the eggs and milk. Follow the same procedure for shaping and baking the biscuits.

Other cheeses (Cheddar, provolone, smoked) and herbs (rosemary, oregano, sage, thyme) may also be used.

49 Butter Kuchen

A yeasted coffee cake not requiring any kneading: tender, moist, and appealing.

> ¼ cup lukewarm water
> 1 tablespoon dry yeast
> ⅓ cup brown sugar
> 1 cup milk
> 1 teaspoon salt
> ¼ cup butter OR margarine
> 2 eggs
> 3¼ cups unbleached white or whole wheat flour

For the topping:

> ½ cup butter
> ½ cup brown sugar
> 1 cup unbleached white or whole wheat flour
> 1 tablespoon cinnamon

[Serves 4–6]

Combine the water with the dry yeast and 1 tablespoon of the sugar, and set aside.

Scald the milk, remove from the heat, and pour into a bowl. Add the rest of the sugar along with the salt and butter or margarine. Once the mixture has cooled to body temperature, stir in the dissolved yeast.

Beat the eggs with ½ cup of the flour. Then add the remainder of the flour to the eggs alternately with the milk–yeast mixture, stirring well after each addition.

Pour batter into a 9- by 13-inch greased pan (or a greased tube pan) and let rise for 45 minutes.

Sprinkle on the butter topping, made by cutting together the topping ingredients.

Bake at 375° for 30 minutes, or until the edges pull away from the sides of the pan and the middle is dry when tested with a toothpick.

50 Egg Bagels

Bagels are a lot of work, but fun to make. This dough can also be made into braided bread, or challah. If you have questions about making a yeasted dough, see "Detailed Instructions," page 15.

I. 1½ cups lukewarm water
    1 package dry yeast
    ¼ cup sugar
    3 eggs, well beaten
    3 cups unbleached white flour

II. ½ cup oil
    2 teaspoons salt
    2–3 cups whole wheat or unbleached white flour

[Makes 12 bagels]

Dissolve the yeast in the lukewarm water. Stir in the sugar, eggs, and unbleached white flour, and beat well. Cover and set aside to rise for 30 minutes. (For onion bagels, add 1 small, diced raw onion.)

Fold in the oil and salt. Then fold in the remaining flour ½ cup or so at a time until the dough comes away from the sides of the bowl. Turn out onto a floured board and knead for 5 minutes. Cover and let rise for 50 minutes. Punch down the dough and let rise another 30 minutes.

Cut the dough into thirds and shape each piece into a ball. (Cover the dough balls you are not working with with a plastic bag or a moist towel to keep a crust from forming.) Cut the first ball into 12 pieces. Roll each piece into a tube, shape the tube around your first two fingers, and connect the ends together by rolling them beneath your fingers on the table.

After you have finished all 12, dip each ring into boiling water for 10 seconds, to develop that genuine bagel crust.

Place the bagels on a greased cookie sheet, allowing them a little elbow room. Brush with Egg Wash (#18) and sprinkle with sesame or poppy seeds, or leave plain. Let rise for 20 minutes.

Bake at 425° for 20 minutes or until golden brown.

Repeat the entire process with the second portion of dough. The third portion can be made into more bagels or a braided bread.

To make a braided bread, divide the dough into six portions. Roll each into a strand and braid (see the illustration for braiding six strands on page 57). Place on a greased sheet and let rise for 25–30 minutes. Brush with Egg Wash and sprinkle with poppy seeds. Bake at 375° for 45–50 minutes or until golden brown.

5 I Walnut Coffee Cake

A sugary, unyeasted coffee cake with a smooth texture, beautifully laced with cinnamon-nut topping.

1/2 cup butter
1 cup sugar
2 eggs
2 1/2 cups cake flour
1 teaspoon baking soda
1 1/2 teaspoons baking powder
1/4 teaspoon salt
1 1/2 cups sour cream with 1 teaspoon vanilla extract stirred in

Streusel topping:

1 cup chopped walnuts
1/2 cup brown sugar
2–3 teaspoons cinnamon
1 1/2 tablespoons cocoa

Superstreusel:

1 cup chopped walnuts
3/4 cup brown sugar
2 tablespoons cinnamon
4 tablespoons butter
2 tablespoons cocoa

[Makes 1 large coffee cake or 12 servings
Preheat oven to 350°]

To make the streusel: Combine the list of ingredients and work with your fingers until the mixture resembles coarse meal.

To make the coffee cake:
Cream together the butter and sugar. Add the eggs one at a time and beat well after each addition. In a separate bowl, sift the flour together with the soda, baking powder, and salt. Add this to the creamed mixture alternately with the sour cream, making about three additions and stirring well after each one.

Spread half of the batter into a large buttered tube pan and sprinkle with half of the streusel. Spread the rest of the batter on next, and finish with the rest of the streusel. Bake the coffeecake for approximately 45 minutes at 350° or until a toothpick comes out clean. Let it cool in the pan, or remove the sides and serve warm.

Muffins &
Quick Breads

Muffins & Quick Breads

Muffins are wonderfully quick and easy to prepare, and generally they require only 20 minutes or so to bake. Plus, people are fond of muffins—at least I am.

Muffins are made by lightly combining wet ingredients—egg, milk, oil, and honey or molasses—with dry ingredients—flour, baking powder, salt. Mixing just until the dry ingredients are moistened (leaving a few lumps) will assure muffins of light, tender, even texture. Overmixing will make the muffins tough and chewy.

Quick breads are generally sweeter than muffins and intended more for desserts than as part of a meal. They are usually baked in loaf pans and are done when a toothpick or fork inserted in the center of the loaf comes out dry. Also, the bread will have begun to pull away from the sides of the pan and will be springy when pressed gently in the center.

A quick-bread batter may also be baked in muffin tins, with a reduced baking time. Muffin batters may be baked in bread pans, in which case the baking time is increased.

52 Jalapeño Corn Bread

This spoonbread is filled with the fresh flavor of corn accented with peppers or chilis—a hearty addition to a light meal. The milder green chilis (poblano) may be used if jalapeños are not available or if you find them too hot. This bread is excellent served with Roasted Garlic and Hot Chili Butter (#82).

2 tablespoons butter
1 cup white or yellow cornmeal
1 teaspoon salt
1½ teaspoons baking soda
1 cup fresh corn with ½ cup cream stirred into it
¾ cup milk
⅓ cup olive oil
3 eggs
⅓ cup roasted, peeled, and chopped jalapeño peppers
1 cup grated sharp Cheddar or Jack cheese

[Serves 6–8
Preheat oven to 400°]

Use a black 9-inch skillet or 1½-quart earthenware casserole to melt the butter in a 400° oven. Meanwhile, combine the dry ingredients, then stir in the fresh corn, milk, oil, eggs, peppers and half of the grated cheese. Remove the baking dish from the oven and pour the batter into it. Distribute the remaining cheese on top and bake for 35 minutes. Best served very hot.

To spice the bread up, add 1 teaspoon cayenne to the dry ingredients.

53 Three-Layer Corn Bread

This bread was invented quite by accident—by mistakenly adding more egg and milk than usual. One batter makes three layers. The cornmeal settles, the bran rises, in the middle is an egg-custardy layer. Easy, glorious, and amazing!

1 cup cornmeal (coarse-ground works best)
½ cup whole wheat flour
½ cup unbleached white flour
¼ cup wheat bran OR wheat germ

2 teaspoons baking powder
1 teaspoon salt
2 eggs
¼–½ cup honey OR *molasses*
¼ cup oil OR *melted butter*
3 cups milk OR *buttermilk*

[Preheat oven to 350°]

Combine the dry ingredients. In a separate bowl, combine the wet ingredients. Mix together. The resulting batter will be quite liquidy.

Pour batter into a greased 9- by 9-inch pan. Bake at 350° for 50 minutes or until the top is springy when gently touched.

As a variation, add a cup of grated cheese—I like Jack, provolone, or Parmesan.

54 Blue Cornmeal Muffins

Blue cornmeal comes from blue corn, grown in the Southwest by the Hopi, who talk and sing to each plant. If you come across some of this blue cornmeal, great, but the recipe can also be made with yellow or white cornmeal. And see what a difference it makes to talk and sing to each muffin. Your heart goes out to things, and things come home to your heart.

1 cup blue cornmeal
2 cups unbleached white flour
4 teaspoons baking powder
½ teaspoon salt
¼ cup sugar
1 cup milk
3 eggs, well beaten
¼ cup melted butter

[Makes 12 very large or 18 smaller muffins
Preheat oven to 400°]

Mix together the cornmeal, flour, baking powder, salt, and sugar. Combine the milk, eggs, and melted butter. Fold the dry ingredients into the wet until just barely moistened. Spoon into greased muffin tins and bake in a 400° oven for 12–15 minutes or until lightly browned on top.

55 Whole Wheat Muffins

Here is a basic whole wheat muffin recipe followed by a number of possible variations. Take your pick or dream up your own.

2 cups whole wheat flour
2 teaspoons baking powder
½ teaspoon salt
1 egg, beaten
¼ cup oil OR *melted butter*
¼–½ cup honey OR *molasses*
1½ cups milk

[Makes 12 large muffins]

Combine the dry ingredients. In a separate bowl combine the wet ingredients. Fold the wet and dry ingredients together with as few strokes as possible, just until the flour is moistened, leaving a few lumps. Spoon into greased muffin tins and bake at 400° for about 15 minutes.

56 Something Missing Muffins

Is everybody a yuppie with kitchen cupboard well stocked and fully supplied? I thought not. After much deliberation I finally decided to leave these recipes in the revised edition, so that, even with something missing, you can still make muffins. Some are more "muffiny" than others—the more they resemble the basic whole wheat muffin recipe. Generally, muffins rise more when sweetened rather than unsweetened, when made with milk rather than water and with baking powder rather than without.

A. Substantial muffins

2 cups whole wheat flour
½ teaspoon salt
2½ cups water OR *milk*

[Makes 12 not large but hefty muffins]

Proceed as for Whole Wheat Muffins (#55), being careful not to overmix.

B. Still quite chewable

2 cups whole wheat flour
½ teaspoon salt

¼ cup oil OR melted butter
2¼ cups water OR milk

[Makes 12 heavy muffins]

Proceed as for Whole Wheat Muffins (#55).

C. A surprisingly light muffin when made with milk, but don't expect too much.

2 cups whole wheat flour
¾ teaspoon salt
¼ cup oil
¼ cup honey OR molasses
2 cups milk OR water

[Makes 12 somewhat tender muffins]

Proceed as for Whole Wheat Muffins (#55).

D. All that's missing is the egg.

2 cups whole wheat flour
¾ teaspoon salt
2 teaspoons baking powder
¼ cup oil OR melted butter
¼ cup honey OR molasses
2 cups milk OR water

[Makes 12 pretty good, nonperfect muffins]

Proceed as for Whole Wheat Muffins (#55).

57 Festival Spice Muffins

A delicious whole wheat muffin, almost a cupcake.

½ teaspoon cinnamon
½ teaspoon mace
¼ teaspoon nutmeg
¼ teaspoon allspice
¼ teaspoon ginger

[Makes 12 large, festive muffins]

Add these spices to the dry ingredients for Whole Wheat Muffins (#55), and proceed with that recipe.

58 "Oriental" Spice Muffins

Another spiced-up muffin with exotic pretensions.

> *½ teaspoon cinnamon*
> *½ teaspoon cardamom (best freshly ground)*
> *¼ teaspoon ground cloves*
> *¼ teaspoon freshly grated nutmeg*
> *¼ teaspoon ginger*

[Makes 12 large, inscrutable muffins]

Add these spices to the dry ingredients for Whole Wheat Muffins (#55), and proceed with that recipe.

59 Fruit Juice Muffins

Different colors and subtle flavors.

Use fruit juice in place of the milk in Whole Wheat Muffins (#55). Other sweetening may be reduced or omitted. (For a really colorful effect, food coloring is necessary.)

[Makes 12 large, strangely tinted muffins]

Proceed with the basic recipe.

60 Marmalade or Jam Muffins

The marmalade or jam gives these muffins some unusual flavor variation.

Use ½ cup marmalade or jam in place of other sweetening in the basic recipe for Whole Wheat Muffins (#55), and proceed with that recipe.

[Makes 12 large, succulent muffins]

61 Dried Fruit Muffins

The dried fruit makes these muffins chewy and sweet.

½ cup raisins
                OR
½ cup chopped dates
                OR
½ cup chopped dried apricots

[Makes 12 large, fruity muffins]

Make the recipe for Whole Wheat Muffins (#55), adding one of the varieties of dried fruit above.

62 *Nut or Seed Muffins*

The full, intense flavor of nuts or seeds enlivens these muffins.

½–¾ cup chopped walnuts
                OR
¼–¾ cup chopped almonds
                OR
½–¾ cup chopped cashews
                OR
½–¾ cup sunflower seeds
                OR
½–¾ cup roasted sesame seeds (roasted in oven or frying pan)

[Makes 12 large, nutty muffins]

In addition to the regular ingredients in Whole Wheat Muffins (#55), add any of the above. The nuts are more flavorful if lightly roasted before adding to the muffin batter. The sesame seeds, because they are so small, are difficult to chew, and roasting makes them easier to bite into. Proceed as in the basic recipe.

63 *Confusion Muffins*

To go beyond the confines of the recipe may cause confusion or delight. Ready or not!

Combine any or all of the variations, or make up you own, and proceed as in the recipe for Whole Wheat Muffins (#55).

[Makes 12 large, festive, inscrutable, fruity, succulent, nutty muffins]

64 Corn Muffins

These are particularly adaptable to seasoning, so I have listed a number of options. The same batter can, of course, be baked in a pan for corn bread.

> *1 cup whole wheat flour*
> *1 cup fine cornmeal*
> *½ teaspoon salt*
> *2 teaspoons baking powder*
> *2 eggs, beaten*
> *¼ cup oil* OR *melted butter*
> *1¼ cups milk*
> *½ teaspoon chili powder (optional)*
> *1 teaspoon dry oregano (optional)*
> *1 teaspoon dry marjoram (optional)*

[Makes 12 muffins
Preheat oven to 400°]

Combine dry ingredients, including your choice of the optional seasonings. Combine wet ingredients and then fold them together with the dry ingredients until just moistened. Spoon into greased muffin tins or a baking pan. Bake at 400° for about 15 minutes for muffins, about 25 minutes for corn bread.

65 Bran Muffins

These muffins have good bran flavor and a light and tender texture. They are good for snacks as well as breakfast.

> *1½ cups unprocessed wheat bran*
> *½ cup boiling water*
> *1¼ cups unbleached white* OR *whole wheat flour*
> *1¼ teaspoons baking soda*
> *¼ teaspoon salt*
> *¼ cup butter*
> *¼ cup sugar*
> *¼ cup molasses*
> *2 eggs*
> *1 cup buttermilk*
> *¾ cup raisins*

[Makes 12 medium-to-large branny muffins
Preheat oven to 400°]

Combine ½ cup of the bran with the boiling water and let it steep. Combine the remaining bran with the rest of the dry ingredients.

In a separate bowl cream the butter and sugar, then blend in the molasses and eggs.

Mix the steeped bran in with the buttermilk.

Add the dry ingredients to the butter–sugar mixture alternately with the buttermilk, beginning and ending with flour and mixing briefly after each addition.

Let the batter stand in the refrigerator for 12 hours. Spoon into greased muffin tins and bake in a 400° oven for 18–25 minutes.

The batter will keep refrigerated up to 3 weeks.

66 Barley Flour Muffins

These are moist and somewhat heavy but have a wonderful nutty flavor.

2 cups barley flour
2 teaspoons baking powder
½ teaspoon salt
¼ cup honey
2 cups milk
¼ cup oil
½ teaspoon vanilla extract

[Makes 12 muffins
Preheat oven to 400°]

Combine the dry ingredients. In a separate bowl combine the wet ingredients. Fold the dry and wet ingredients together, until the flour is just moistened. Spoon into oiled muffin tins. Bake 20 minutes at 400°.

67 Carrot Cake

Here is our bakery's version of an old standard: rich with butter, oil, and sugar; richly scented with cinnamon, allspice, and nutmeg; and richly filled with carrots, raisins, and nuts. Rich, rich, rich—yet it tastes so wholesome.

1 cup white sugar
1 cup brown sugar
4 eggs
⅔ cup melted butter
⅔ cup oil
2 cups unbleached white OR *whole wheat flour*
1 tablespoon cinnamon
2 teaspoons allspice
2 teaspoons freshly grated nutmeg
1 cup chopped walnuts
3 cups grated carrots
1 cup raisins (dark or golden)

[One 10-inch tube pan or two 8-inch layer pans
Preheat oven to 350°]

Mix the two sugars and cream them with the eggs. Mix in the melted butter and oil. In a separate bowl, mix the flour, spices, and chopped nuts. Blend this mixture thoroughly into the sugar mixture. Stir in the carrots and raisins.

Put into a well-buttered and -floured 10-inch tube pan. Bake in a 350° oven for 1 hour and 10 minutes. This cake may also be baked in two 8-inch layers. In this case, bake only for 30–35 minutes.

Let cake cool, and remove from the pan. Sift a little powdered sugar over it or crown it with Cream Cheese Icing (#109).

68 Apple Nut Loaf (Yeasted)

Scented with vanilla, zested with orange peel, moist and fruity.

2 tablespoons yeast
½ cup sweet cider (lukewarm)
1 cup honey
½ cup oil
4 eggs, beaten
½ teaspoon salt
2 teaspoons vanilla extract
2 tablespoons finely chopped orange peel
4 cups whole wheat flour
4 cups grated raw apples with skins
1 cup coarsely chopped nuts (no peanuts)

Optional:

1 tablespoon cinnamon
1 teaspoon allspice
1 teaspoon nutmeg
½ cup coconut
½ cup dates or raisins

[Makes 2 large loaves]

Soften the yeast in the cider. Blend together the honey, oil, eggs, salt, and flavorings. Add the yeast mixture, and then stir in the flour, apples, and nuts, as well as any of the optional ingredients.

Turn into oiled loaf pans. Let rise for one hour, and then bake at 350°–375° for 45–60 minutes until nicely browned.

ana Nut Bread

This bread has a higher proportion of banana pulp than most, which gives the bread a full banana flavor but also makes it less caky. Good for dessert, it can also be toasted for breakfast.

> 2 cups whole wheat flour
> 1 teaspoon baking soda
> ~~1/4 teaspoon salt~~
> 1/2 cup butter OR oil
> 1/2 cup sugar OR honey
> ~~grated rind of 1 lemon~~
> 2 eggs, beaten
> 2 cups banana pulp (~~6~~ 3-4 small ones)
> 1/2 cup chopped walnuts or almonds
> 1/2 cup raisins (optional)

[Makes 1 large loaf
Preheat oven to 350°]

Sift together the flour, soda, and salt. Cream the butter and sugar (or blend the oil and honey), then beat in the lemon peel and eggs. Add the sifted ingredients in three parts alternately with the banana pulp, beating smooth after each addition. Fold in the chopped nuts (and raisins if using them).

Place the batter in a greased loaf pan and bake for about 50 60 minutes at 350° or until a toothpick inserted in the center comes out dry. Cool for 5 minutes before removing from the pan.

70 Honey Walnut Bread

Milk and honey—there's nothing quite like it. Honey Walnut Bread is fragrant and has a fine crumb.

> 1 cup milk
> 1 cup honey
> 1/2 cup soft butter
> 2 eggs, beaten
> 2 1/2 cups whole wheat flour (or 1/2 white and 1/2 whole wheat)
> 1 teaspoon salt
> 1 tablespoon baking powder
> 1/2–3/4 cup chopped walnuts

Combine the milk and honey, and stir over low heat until blended. Remove from the heat and beat in the butter, eggs, flour, salt, and baking powder. Mix until well blended. Fold in the nuts.

Place in a greased loaf pan, and bake for 1 hour at 325°, or until a toothpick comes out clean. Cool for 15 minutes in the pan before removing. Let cool longer before slicing.

71 Date Nut Bread

The recipe may call for whole wheat flour, but this bread is richly spiced and packed with dates and nuts.

> *2 cups whole wheat flour*
> *2 teaspoons baking powder*
> *2 teaspoons cinnamon*
> *½ teaspoon mace*
> *½ teaspoon salt*
> *6 tablespoons butter*
> *½ cup brown sugar*
> *2 eggs, well beaten*
> *½ cup milk*
> *1 cup chopped dates*
> *½ cup chopped walnuts*
> *2 teaspoons grated orange peel*

[Makes 1 large loaf
Preheat oven to 325°]

Sift together the flour, baking powder, spices, and salt. Cream the butter with the sugar, and beat in the eggs. Add the dry ingredients alternately with the milk, beginning and ending with the dry ingredients. Fold in the dates, nuts, and orange peel.

Place in a greased loaf pan, and bake at 325° for 60 minutes or more until a toothpick comes out clean. Cool 5 minutes in the pan before removing to a wire rack. Serve plain or with butter or cream cheese. Delight in the simple good fortune.

Compound Butters

Compound Butters

This is an entirely new section for the revised edition, inspired by my friend Sammie Daniels, who has a catering business in Inverness, California. Presented here are only a few examples; as you can see, the possibilities are limited only by your imagination. So once you get started, you can experiment on your own.

These compound butters may be used any way you would use plain butter: on hot toast, muffins, pancakes; on bread or sandwiches; with vegetables or eggs.

Hidden flavors emerge. Surprises are in store.

Nut Butters

Nut butters are adaptable to a great many uses, crossing all the boundaries from breakfast to dessert. In addition to being served with morning breads and pastries, they can be rolled up in pancakes with a little powdered sugar sprinkled on top: Almond and Orange Butter in Cottage Cheese Pancakes, for example.

They are excellent tossed with pastas or used as a garnish to perk up soups or steamed vegetables.

They can be served with quick breads: Almond and Orange Butter on Banana Nut Bread or Apple Nut Loaf, Hazelnut Butter on Honey Walnut Bread, Pecan and Ginger Butter on Date Nut Bread.

Or try these butters when making a dessert: Almond and Orange Butter used in making Apple Crisp or Hazelnut Butter in the Peach Kuchen. You get the idea. Or use the Pecan and Ginger Butter to enliven a fresh fruit tart, brushing it on the crust before adding the fresh fruit and glaze.

72 Hazelnut Butter

1 stick sweet butter, softened
1/3–1/2 cup toasted and ground hazelnuts
splash cognac

In a small bowl, combine the butter and the ground nuts. Mix them very well and flavor with a splash of cognac. Roll into a log on waxed paper. Store tightly covered until ready to use.

73 Almond and Orange Butter

1 stick sweet butter, softened
1/3 cup finely ground almonds
2 tablespoons freshly squeezed orange juice
zest of same orange
1 teaspoon sugar
1 teaspoon rum (for zip)

In a small bowl, mix the butter and almonds. Little by little, work in the orange juice, zest, sugar, and rum. Pack into a 1-cup ramekin and store covered in the refrigerator.

74 Pecan and Ginger Butter

1 stick sweet butter, softened
1/2 cup very finely ground pecans
1 1/2 tablespoons very finely minced crystallized ginger
1 teaspoon brown sugar (optional)
1/2 teaspoon allspice (optional)

In a small bowl, mix the butter and pecans. Stir in the ginger and then taste. Add the remaining ingredients, or add more ginger or both. Chill in a ramekin. Keeps at cool room temperature.

Sweet Butters

Try these sweet butters in the morning with toast, muffins, bagels, or breakfast rolls. Heap Chocolate Nutmeg Butter on toasted Country French Bread, or Coffee Liqueur Butter on a Flaky Biscuit. How about Honey Lemon Butter on Lemon Twist Bread or Vanilla Bean Butter on Cream Scones?

75 Honey Lemon Butter

1 stick sweet butter, softened
2 tablespoons honey
juice and zest of 1 medium lemon

Combine all the ingredients and stir well with a fork. Form into a log on waxed paper or chill in a butter mold until ready to use. Well wrapped, this keeps for a week in the refrigerator.

76 Chocolate Nutmeg Butter

1 stick sweet butter, softened
3 tablespoons sweetened cocoa
½ whole nutmeg, grated

Combine all the ingredients in a small bowl and mix well. Form into a log and roll in waxed paper. Chill until hard, then unwrap and cut into bite-sized pieces.

77 Vanilla Bean Butter

1 stick sweet butter, softened
2 vanilla beans, soaked in hot water for 20 minutes
3–4 tablespoons sifted powdered sugar or more to taste

In a small bowl, combine the butter and the scrapings only from the vanilla beans. Mix well and sift in the powdered sugar. Chill in a pretty mold and serve on a plate.

78 Coffee Liqueur Butter

1 stick sweet butter, softened
2 tablespoons instant coffee powder
2 tablespoons Kahlua or coffee liqueur
powdered sugar to taste

In a small bowl, combine the butter and coffee powder. Blend in the liqueur and some sifted sugar to taste. Form into a log on waxed paper or put into a mold. Chill.

Savory Butters

The savory butters, like the nut butters, are versatile: use them to accompany breads, garnish soups, and flavor vegetables or pasta dishes. Spread on little toasts, they can be used to garnish and float in a bowl of soup. Try the Roasted Garlic and Hot Chili Butter on the Jalapeño Cornbread. The Lemon Mustard Butter is always great on a sandwich. The Lime and Cilantro Butter is wonderful on tortillas or with Corn Muffins. The Balsamic Butter is delicious spread on rye bread.

79 Balsamic Butter

> *4 tablespoons balsamic vinegar*
> *2 tablespoons red wine*
> *6 tablespoons sweet butter*
> *salt & pepper*

In a saucepan, combine the vinegar and wine and reduce by half. Beat in the butter 1 tablespoon at a time until a thick emulsion develops. Season with salt and pepper. Serve warm, or chill in a small dish and use like cold butter.

80 Lemon Mustard Butter

> *1 stick sweet butter, softened*
> *1½ tablespoons Dijon mustard*
> *1–2 tablespoons fresh lemon juice*
> *salt & white pepper to taste*

With a fork, cream together the butter, mustard, and lemon juice. Taste; then add some salt and pepper. Shape into a log on a piece of waxed paper or clear plastic. Wrap and chill. When hard, cut into ¼-inch pieces to serve.

81 Lime and Cilantro Butter

1½ sticks sweet butter
juice and zest of one lime
½ cup chopped fresh cilantro
salt & pepper to taste

In a small bowl, combine all the ingredients. Form into a log on waxed paper or plastic or put into a butter mold. Chill until ready to use, then cut off small pieces and arrange on a plate.

82 Roasted Garlic and Hot Chili Butter

1½ sticks salted butter, softened
3 cloves garlic, oven-roasted in their skins until quite soft
1½ teaspoons red pepper flakes
salt to taste

Place the butter in a small bowl. Squeeze the cooked garlic cloves from their skins and mash well into the butter, adding the red pepper to taste. Add a little salt as necessary. Roll into a log on a piece of waxed paper. Chill until hard. Serve on anything you want to spice up. Good in soups, too.

Desserts

Desserts

A good dessert makes a celebration of any occasion. Not that we have to treat ourselves royally every day, but offering dessert with generosity and warmth, we can appreciate the bounty of our lives and celebrate a moment of aliveness.

Once upon a time we were not really into desserts, were we? We put up with them, begrudgingly or at a distance. Sugar, we said, rots the body and mind. Well, times change. We have stopped depriving ourselves of real desserts and congratulating ourselves for our forbearance. No sugar, no enlightenment.

Now, I do not mean to encourage people to become sugar junkies, and I myself cannot eat sugar at the rate I used to and still function with clarity and alertness. But I am also not going to scold people for eating a dessert that is really a dessert. Every moment is a gateway to the truth. Which way is in? Which way is out? Are you entering or leaving?

So the long and short of it is that this section of the book has been greatly expanded from the first edition. I have added several recipes from our Tassajara Bread Bakery in San Francisco, including Chocolate Mousse Pie and Triple Chocolate Cake, as well as some other very pleasant cookies and cakes.

May all beings be healthy, happy, free from suffering.

And may desserts celebrate our wondrous nature. Fully.

KITCHEN PRICES
Listening to Advice $15.00
Giving Advice $15.00
Arguments $25.00
Hugs and Kisses for free only

83 Cheesecake Cookies

I always liked these cookies because they are quick to make, are beautiful, and serve more people than an equivalent amount of cheesecake.

> 1 cup whole wheat flour
> 1/3 cup brown sugar
> 1/3 cup butter OR margarine
> 1/2 cup chopped walnuts OR toasted sesame seeds OR roasted
>   sunflower seeds
> 8 ounces cream cheese
> 1/4 cup honey
> 1 egg
> 2 tablespoons milk
> 1 tablespoon lemon juice
> grated peel of 1 lemon
> 1/2 teaspoon vanilla extract
> 1/2 teaspoon freshly grated nutmeg (optional)
> Garnish (optional):
>   fruit slices: orange, apple, banana, strawberries
>   nutmeats (whole or chopped): almonds, walnuts, Brazil nuts

[Makes 16 2-inch-square cookies
Preheat oven to 350°]

Blend together the flour, sugar, and butter with a pastry cutter to make a crumbly texture, then mix in the 1/2 cup chopped walnuts. Reserve 1/2 cup of the mixture for the topping, and press the remainder into an oiled 8-inch square pan. Bake at 350° for 12–15 minutes.

In the meantime soften the cream cheese and blend in the honey, egg, milk, lemon juice and peel, and seasonings. Spread over the baked crust and sprinkle on the reserved topping. Garnish, if you wish, with fruit slices and/or nutmeats. Bake at 350° for 25 minutes. Cool and cut into 2-inch squares.

Note: If using strawberries for garnish, put them on the cheesecake topping after baking.

84 Turkish Coffee Cake Cookie Bars

Here is another of my old favorites, quick to make and delicious to eat.
Chocolate chips can be put between the layers if you like.

2 cups whole wheat flour
1 cup brown sugar
2 tablespoons Turkish-type coffee OR powdered instant coffee
2 teaspoons cinnamon
½ teaspoon freshly grated nutmeg
¼ teaspoon allspice OR ground coriander (optional)
½ cup butter OR margarine
1 cup sour cream
1 egg, beaten
1 teaspoon baking soda
½ cup chopped nuts
4 ounces chocolate chips (optional)

[Makes 24 1½- by 3-inch bars
Preheat oven to 350°]

Mix together the flour, sugar, coffee, and spices, then cut in the butter
with a pastry cutter until crumbly. Press half of this mixture into a 9- by
13-inch pan. Mix the remaining half with the sour cream, egg, soda,
and chopped nuts. If using chocolate chips, sprinkle them over the crust
in the pan. Pour the batter on top of the crust. Bake at 350° for 25–30
minutes, until the middle is springy.

85 Honey Bars

I have always loved the soft but chewy texture of these bars and the exquisite bouquet of spices, honey, and fruit peel. They can be kept for several weeks in a tightly closed tin.

> 1½ cups honey
> 3 tablespoons butter OR margarine
> 2 cups whole wheat flour, sifted with 1 tablespoon baking powder
> 2 tablespoons chopped lemon or orange peel OR 1 tablespoon
>   of each
> 2 teaspoons cinnamon
> ½ teaspoon freshly ground cardamom
> ¼ teaspoon ground cloves
> ¼ teaspoon mace OR allspice OR ground coriander (optional)
> ½ cup chopped almonds or other nuts
> 1½–2 cups whole wheat flour

> [Makes about 24 large bars
> Preheat oven to 350°]

Have all the ingredients ready to mix quickly before the mixture stiffens with cooling.

Heat the honey in a saucepan slowly just until liquidy; remove from the heat. Stir in the butter or margarine and then the sifted flour with baking powder to make a thick batter. Add the fruit peel, spices, and nuts, and then add the additional flour until a dough forms.

Pat the dough into a buttered pan until you have a layer ⅜ inch thick. Bake at 350° for about 20–25 minutes. Be careful not to overbake or the cookies will be quite hard. When done, the bottoms will be lightly browned and the tops dry but not browned.

Remove from the pan while still warm and slice into bars. Then cool before storing.

Variation: To make more of a "fruitcake" honey bar, add ¼ cup each of chopped citron and chopped candied orange or chopped lemon peel along with the spices and nuts.

86 Date Bars

These can be whipped up in just a few minutes and eaten in about the same length of time or lingered over indefinitely. Raisins, figs, or prunes can be substituted for dates.

3 eggs
½ cup brown sugar
1 teaspoon vanilla extract
1 cup whole wheat flour
1 teaspoon baking powder
⅛ teaspoon salt
½ teaspoon ground cloves
1 teaspoon cinnamon
½ teaspoon allspice
1 cup chopped dates OR *raisins* OR *figs* OR *prunes*
½ cup chopped nutmeats

[Makes 18–24 bars
Preheat oven to 325°]

Beat eggs until light. Gradually blend in the brown sugar along with the vanilla. Sift together the flour, baking powder, salt, and spices, add them to the eggs, and beat until well blended. Fold in the fruit and nutmeats. Pour into a buttered and floured 9- by 13-inch pan and bake at 325° for 20–25 minutes.

87 Tassajara Shortbread

This shortbread may be quickly pressed into the bottom of a tart pan or made into cookies. These light, little cookies can be topped with pecan halves or dipped in chocolate. Simple, but delightful.

1 cup salted butter
½ cup powdered sugar
2 cups unbleached white flour
splash vanilla extract

[Preheat oven to 350°]

Cream together the butter and sugar. Mix in the flour and perhaps a little vanilla. Press into the bottom of a 10-inch tart pan with removable sides. Bake at 350° for 25–30 minutes. Remove from the oven, cut into squares while still hot, and allow to cool. This shortbread will keep for several weeks in a tin.

To make the shortbread into cookies, roll the dough into a log about 2 inches in diameter. Wrap in waxed paper or plastic and refrigerate for 20–30 minutes before slicing into cookies. Place on an ungreased cookie sheet and bake at 350° for about 20 minutes.

For pecan shortbreads, place a pecan half on each cookie before baking.

For chocolate shortbreads, dip the top of the already-baked cookies in melted bittersweet or semisweet chocolate or in one of the chocolate glazes (#104 or #105).

88 Lemon Bars

Uncommonly lemony, simple, and quick to prepare, this recipe from our bakery provides a crisp tartness in a refreshing, light dessert.

For the shortbread crust:

1¼ cups flour
¼ cup sugar
⅔ cup butter, chilled and cut into ½-tablespoon pieces

To prepare the crust, work the flour, sugar, and butter together until they form a dough. Press this into an 8-inch round or square pan. Bake in a 325° oven for 20 minutes.

For the lemon filling:

⅔ cup sugar
2 teaspoons baking powder
½ cup fresh lemon juice
2 eggs
zest of 1 lemon

Prepare the filling while the shortbread is baking. Whisk together the sugar, baking powder, lemon juice, and eggs along with the zest. Pour this mixture over the baked crust and continue baking another 30 minutes or until slightly browned on top. After it cools, sift a little powdered sugar on top, if you like. Cut into squares.

89 Walnut Cookies

Another one of our bakery favorites.

1 cup softened butter
2¼ cups unbleached white flour
⅓ cup brown sugar
1 teaspoon vanilla extract
⅔ cup finely chopped walnuts
powdered sugar

[Makes approximately 18 cookies
Preheat oven to 350°]

Reserve ¼ cup of the flour and then combine all ingredients in the order listed. Add the reserved flour as necessary until the dough comes away from the sides of the bowl.

Form into balls 1½ inches in diameter and place on a well-greased baking sheet 2 inches apart.

Bake at 350° until firm to the touch, about 20 minutes. After baking, the cookies may be tossed in powdered sugar.

90 Italian Cookies

Scented but not too sweet, dryish and crunchy but not too tough, these cookies are great for coffee-dipping or tea-dunking.

1 cup sweet butter
2 cups sugar
2 eggs
4 cups unbleached white flour
2 teaspoons baking powder
2 teaspoons anise extract
1⅓ tablespoons orange extract

[Makes approximately 30 cookies
Preheat oven to 350°]

Cream together the butter and sugar. Beat in the eggs. Then mix in the flour and baking powder. Add the anise and orange extracts and blend thoroughly. Divide the dough into four equal pieces, shape into flat-bottomed logs, and put two each on well-greased baking sheets. Bake in a 350° oven until a toothpick comes out clean. Baking time varies with the thickness of the logs. Check them after 30 minutes. Cut the logs while still warm into 1-inch pieces and let them cool completely. They keep well in a tin.

91 Coconut Macaroons

Intensely sweet and coconutty, these macaroons can satisfy any sweet tooth, especially when they are dipped in chocolate, as in the variation.

½ cup egg whites (probably 3)
pinch salt
1½ cups sugar
¾ teaspoon vanilla extract
¾ teaspoon almond extract
2 tablespoons flour
14 ounces dry, unsweetened coconut

Beat egg whites with salt until soft peaks form. Gradually add the sugar, continuing to beat until stiff. Beat in vanilla and almond extracts. Fold in flour and coconut until thoroughly incorporated.

Drop very large spoonfuls at least 2 inches apart, onto a greased baking sheet.

Bake in a slow oven, 300°–325°, until firm and slightly golden. Remove the macaroons from the sheet while still hot and cool them on a rack.

For chocolate coconut macaroons: Melt 2 ounces of bittersweet chocolate over a slow flame and stir until melted. Dip the bottoms of the macaroons in the melted chocolate and turn upside down to dry.

92 Nutty Gritty Cookies

Revised to work! These cookies are crunchy with cornmeal, millet meal, bread crumbs, nuts, and seeds. They are not particularly stylish or sweet, but are full of good old grit and wholesome country flavors.

½ cup oil
½ cup honey
2 cups bread crumbs (or ½ cup whole wheat flour)
1½ teaspoons salt
1 cup sesame seeds, roasted (dry-roast in pan or oven)
1 cup sunflower seeds, roasted
1 cup rolled oats, lightly roasted
1 cup walnuts, lightly roasted
1 cup cracked millet
1 cup fine cornmeal
1 cup raisins
water as needed

[Makes a bunch
Preheat oven to 350°]

Blend the oil and honey together, then mix in the remaining ingredients except for the water. Add water a little at a time until the mixture holds together. If the mixture gets too wet, add some more flour. Shape into balls and place on a lightly oiled cookie sheet. Bake at 350° for about 25 minutes.

93 Fresh Fruit Cake

This is an unusual cake, made without eggs, baking powder, sugar, or honey. The texture is dense yet soft and crumbly. I have not tried this with flours other than wheat, but they would probably work fairly well (for those with wheat allergies).

1 cup oil
1 cup nut pieces
1 cup raisins
1 cup coconut
2 cups rolled oats
3 cups crushed fruit (pulp and juice)
½ teaspoon salt
1 teaspoon vanilla extract
2–2½ cups whole wheat flour

[Makes 2 9-inch rounds
Preheat oven to 350°]

For the crushed fruit, use strawberries, other berries, pineapple, banana, apricot, peaches, nectarines. The fruit may be coarsely chopped or blended to a purée. Apples or pears may also be used if first cooked and made into sauce, or grated with juice added for liquid.

Mix together all the ingredients except for the wheat flour. Then add the flour to form a soft, slightly crumbly dough. The amount of flour will vary with the moisture content of the fruit.

Press or spread into buttered pans and bake in a 350° oven for 40–50 minutes until the sides and bottom are golden brown. (Take a peek.) Let cool in the pans for 10 minutes before turning out onto a plate or board for further cooling. Frost with a date filling, decorated with pieces of fresh fruit.

To make the date filling, place ½ pound pitted dates in a saucepan with water to cover and simmer for 10–15 minutes until the dates are soft. Mash into a paste or whip in a blender, and season with lemon or orange peel.

94 Haver Cookies

One of our no-sugar, no-honey classics, this recipe makes a chewy but not tough "cookie." A good, wholesome snack food with excellent grain flavors.

½ cup currants or raisins
1¼ cups rolled oats
2 teaspoons cinnamon
½ teaspoon salt
2 tablespoons corn oil
½ cup whole wheat flour
½ cup unbleached white flour
5–7 tablespoons apple juice

[Makes about 24
Preheat oven to 350°]

Soak raisins in water for ½ hour. Combine oats, cinnamon, and salt. Add oil, stir thoroughly, and set aside. Mix flours and juice. Add the oat mixture and then the drained raisins. If the mixture does not hold together, add extra teaspoons of oil or juice until it does.

Shape the mixture into a ball and place it on a large greased baking sheet. Roll the dough with a heavy rolling pin into a large rectangle ¼ inch thick. Using a sharp knife, cut across the dough to form rectangular strips 3–4 inches wide. Then cut zigzag fashion across each rectangle to form triangles.

Bake the Havers at 350° for 20–30 minutes. Do not brown. Let cool and remove from the pan. Store in a tin.

95 Sesame Candy (Halvah)

To make this homemade halvah you will need some way to grind the sesame seeds—a Corona handmill, an electric blender, a Japanese suribachi. After that, it is simple to sweeten and spice.

> 2 cups unhulled sesame seeds
> 1 tablespoon sesame oil (optional)
> ¼ cup or more honey OR sugar
> 2 tablespoons butter OR margarine OR tahini
> Spices (optional, to taste):
>   1 teaspoon vanilla extract
>   ¼ teaspoon cloves
>   ½ teaspoon cinnamon
>   ¼ teaspoon cardamom OR coriander OR nutmeg OR mace

[Makes 6–8 healthy but moderate servings]

Roast the seeds until they are crunchy—in a frying pan over a moderate flame or on a baking sheet in the oven. Stir often enough that they roast evenly. Grind the seeds finely, but not so finely that you end up with sesame butter. Add the sweetening and the butter (and the sesame oil if using it). Taste. The basic recipe is not very sweet, so you may well wish to add more honey or sugar and some vanilla. If you want the halvah to have some spiciness, take your pick of the spices and season to taste. Shape into balls and roll in toasted sesame seeds, or press onto a cookie sheet and refrigerate before slicing.

96 Raw Fruit Carob Candy

Still trying to be good and not eat chocolate? Or you just really love the flavor of carob? Here is a way to enjoy carob without sugar or oils.

> 2 cups pitted dates
> 1 cup seedless raisins
> ½ cup chopped walnuts (optional)
> carob powder
> ½ cup sesame seeds, toasted

Grind the dates and raisins together or chop them to a coarse paste. Add the walnuts if using them. Add as much carob powder as the mixture will hold. Shape into balls and roll the balls in roasted sesame seeds.

Variation: Mix 1 cup of roasted, ground sesame seeds with the dates and raisins before adding the carob powder (sesame halvah carob date raisin candy coming up).

97 Cream Cheese Balls

Here is a simple recipe for a light dessert or tea treat.

> *1 pound cream cheese at room temperature*
> *3/4 cup raisins or chopped dates*
> *whole wheat flour*
> *1/2 cup grated dry unsweetened coconut*
> *1 tablespoon grated lemon or orange rind*
> *1/2 teaspoon allspice*
> *3/4 cup chopped almonds OR sesame seeds OR sunflower seeds*

[Makes 16–24]

Soften the cream cheese. If using dates, mix them with a small amount of whole wheat flour to separate. Blend the raisins or dates, coconut, fruit peel, and allspice in with the cream cheese. Squeeze everything together in your hands and shape into 1-inch balls. Roll the balls in the chopped almonds or toasted seeds.

98 Apple Crisp

From the good old days of Tassajara barbecues—tossed salad, half chickens, pork ribs, French bread, baked potatoes, green beans, corn on the cob, red and white wine—comes a good old dessert.

4–6 pippin apples
juice of 1 lemon
1 teaspoon or more cinnamon
½ teaspoon or more freshly grated nutmeg
¾ cup brown sugar
1 cup whole wheat flour
½ cup butter OR *margarine*
whipped cream, and lots of it

[Serves 6
Preheat oven to 375°]

Wash, quarter, core, and slice the apples, thickly or thinly. Toss with the lemon juice and then arrange in a buttered 9- by 13-inch pan. Sprinkle on the cinnamon and freshly grated nutmeg. Mix the sugar and flour together and cut in the butter or margarine with a pastry cutter until it is in pea-sized lumps. Sprinkle this topping onto the apples.

Bake for about 45 minutes at 375° or until the apples are fork-soft.

Serve plain or topped with whipped cream and a grating of nutmeg. Ice cream will also do—nicely.

Variation: The crisp can also be made with peaches, pears, nectarines, or apricots. Dabbling with other spices is also permitted, though a light hand is advisable.

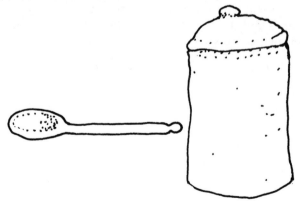

99 Peach Kuchen

A peach-jewel mosaic set in custard baked on a sweet crust.

2 cups flour
¼ teaspoon baking powder
½ teaspoon salt
1 cup brown sugar
½ cup butter
12 skinned peach halves OR 2 packages frozen peach slices (or
    other fruit)
1 teaspoon cinnamon
2 egg yolks, beaten, OR 2 whole eggs
1 cup heavy cream OR sour cream

[Serves 2–12 (Did they eat dinner first?)
Preheat oven to 400°]

Note: To remove the skins from fresh peaches, dip them in boiling water for 10–15 seconds and then peel. If the peaches are not so ripe and the skins are hard to remove, the peaches can be left longer in the boiling water.

Combine flour, baking powder, salt, and 2 tablespoons of the sugar. Cut the butter into the flour mixture with a pastry cutter until it looks like coarse meal. Press this firmly into a baking pan (9 by 13 inches is probably about right). Arrange the peach halves on the surface. Mix the remaining sugar with the cinnamon and sprinkle it over the fruit.

Bake for 15 minutes at 400°, then beat the yolks together with the cream and pour it over the top, and bake an additional 40 minutes at 375° or until the peaches are soft and the custard has thickened.

100 Torte with Sour Cream Fruit Topping

A wonderfully soft, velvety texture, scented with vanilla and mace, makes this an excellent cake to absorb the juices of the fruit and sour cream. This recipe could also be used for strawberry shortcake.

½ teaspoon mace
1 teaspoon vanilla extract
½ cup butter OR margarine
1 cup white sugar
1 cup sifted white flour
½ cup cornstarch
1½ teaspoons baking powder
½ teaspoon salt
2 large eggs, beaten
¼ cup milk

[Serves 6 or more
Preheat oven to 350°]

Blend the mace and vanilla into the butter or margarine. Cream in the sugar. Sift together the flour, cornstarch, baking powder, and salt. Beat the eggs and milk together. Add the dry ingredients to the butter–sugar mixture alternately with the eggs and milk, beginning and ending with the dry ingredients. Mix well after each addition.

Butter and flour a 9-inch cake pan. Add the batter and bake at 350° for 45 minutes or until the center is dry. Cool in the pan for 20 minutes, then turn out onto wire rack. Turn right side up.

For the topping:

2–3 tablespoons honey or sugar
1 cup sour cream
½ teaspoon vanilla extract
fruit

Combine topping ingredients and mix in fruit pieces of the season's choosing.

IOI Mustard Gingerbread

I think of gingerbread as a ho-hum sort of dessert, until I bite into a forkful. The real thing is incomparably better than the thought. Here are directions that could turn into gingerbread—with a helping hand.

2¼ cups sifted whole wheat flour
1½ teaspoons baking powder
½ teaspoon salt
½ teaspoon baking soda
½ teaspoon cloves
1 teaspoon powdered mustard
1 teaspoon cinnamon
1 teaspoon powdered ginger
½ cup butter OR *margarine*
1 cup molasses
1 large egg
1 cup hot water
whipped cream

[Preheat oven to 350°]

Sift together the flour, baking powder, and salt. Blend the soda and spices into the butter or margarine. Gradually blend in the molasses, followed by the egg. Add the flour mixture alternately with the hot water, beginning and ending with the flour and mixing thoroughly after each addition.

Turn into a buttered-and-floured 9-inch square pan or a loaf pan and bake at 350° for 45–50 minutes or until a toothpick comes out clean from the center. Cool in the pan for 10 minutes before turning out to finish cooling. Serve with whipped cream (or applesauce or peach slices).

102 Yogurt Cake

This fine-crumbed, melt-in-the-mouth cake is beautiful served in slices on a large platter with powdered sugar sprinkled over them. It also may be served with fruit and whipped cream, or even toasted for breakfast.

> 1 cup salted butter
> 2 cups sugar
> 5 egg yolks
> 3 cups cake flour, sifted with 1½ teaspoons baking powder and
>   ¼ teaspoon mace
> 1 cup yogurt
> 5 egg whites
> ½ cup sugar
> ¼ teaspoon salt
> ¼ teaspoon cream of tartar   [Serves 12
>   Preheat oven to 350°]

Cream the butter and sugar until fluffy. Beat in the yolks one at a time. Add the flour mixture alternately with the yogurt, beginning and ending with flour.

Beat the egg whites until they form soft peaks, gradually adding the sugar, salt, and cream of tartar.

Fold the whites into the batter. Bake in a greased and floured tube pan at 350° for 50–60 minutes. Test with a toothpick. If it comes out clean, the cake is done.

103 Triple Chocolate Cake

Intense chocolate flavor and melt-in-the-mouth texture make this cake a delicious and satisfying chocolate dessert. Both the cake and the icing are only moderately sweet.

> 5 ounces semisweet chocolate
> 1½ ounces unsweetened chocolate
> ¾ cup butter
> ½ cup white sugar
> 4 egg yolks
> ½ cup cake flour or unbleached white flour
> ½ cup ground almonds
> 4 egg whites
> ⅛ teaspoon cream of tartar
> ¼ cup white sugar

134

Melt chocolates and butter over a very low flame or in a double boiler. Once the chocolate and butter begin to soften, stir until smooth, remove from heat, and set aside to cool.

Beat ½ cup sugar into the yolks until light and lemony in color. Beat in the somewhat cooled chocolate mixture. Stir in the flour and almonds until the flour is dissolved.

Beat the egg whites with the cream of tartar until soft peaks form, then beat in ¼ cup sugar a little at a time until the whites are stiff. Fold one-third of the whites into the batter to lighten it, then carefully fold in the remaining whites so as to maintain as much volume as possible.

To prepare the pan, first butter it, then cut out a sheet of waxed paper to fit the bottom. Butter the waxed paper and dust with flour. Pour the batter into the pan and smooth out the surface.

Bake the cake at 375° in the middle third of the oven for 50 minutes or until the edges have pulled away from the sides and the middle of the cake is springy. Let cool in the pan for 10 minutes and then remove to a rack. When cooled, it may be left plain or iced with Simple Chocolate Glaze (#104).

104 Simple Chocolate Glaze

This icing does not mound up but is thick enough to nicely glaze the Triple Chocolate Cake (#103) or another of your choice.

6 ounces semisweet chocolate
6 ounces butter at room temperature
flavoring (optional): vanilla, brandy, rum, or Grand Marnier

[Glazes a 9- or 10-inch layer]

Melt the chocolate slowly in a double boiler. Remove from heat and work in the butter a little at a time until blended. Add flavoring if desired. Let cool to room temperature before icing the cake.

105 Chocolate Glaze

An easy-to-prepare glaze that will elegantly "choclify" any cake or cookie.

4 ounces bittersweet chocolate
3 tablespoons sugar
3 tablespoons water
3 tablespoons sweet butter

[Enough for 2 medium layers or 1 large cake]

Grate or break up the chocolate and put it in a heavy saucepan with the sugar and the water. Melt slowly over very low heat or in a double boiler. Stir until the chocolate is barely melted, and remove from heat. Stir in the butter 1 tablespoon at a time, until the mixture is satiny-smooth.

Let the glaze continue to cool and thicken to a spreading consistency. Pour over the cake and let it drip down the sides.

106 White Layer Cake or Boston Cream Pie

I know everybody likes chocolate, but I like vanilla, so here it is.

½ cup butter, softened
¾ cup sugar
2 eggs
1½ cups unbleached white flour
2 tablespoons dry milk
2½ teaspoons baking powder
⅝ cup water
1 teaspoon vanilla extract

Cream the butter, then cream in the sugar. Add the eggs one at a time and beat well to blend. Stir in the dry ingredients alternately with the wet, beginning and ending with the dry.

Grease and flour two 8-inch round layer pans and divide the batter between them. Bake at 350° for 20 minutes until golden on top. Let cool in the pans for a few minutes before removing to a cooling rack.

This may be assembled with Vanilla Pastry Cream (#107) between the layers and Buttercream Frosting (#108) on top.

For Boston Cream Pie: Put Vanilla Pastry Cream (#107) between layers and one of the chocolate glazes (#104 or #105) on top.

107 Vanilla Pastry Cream

This pastry cream can be used between layers of cakes or underneath fresh fruit in a tart.

2 tablespoons plus 1 teaspoon cornstarch
1 cup milk
3 egg yolks
⅓ cup sugar
1 tablespoon cream
½ teaspoon vanilla extract

Dissolve cornstarch in a couple of tablespoons of the milk. In a separate bowl, beat the yolks, then whisk in the rest of the milk, the sugar, cream, and vanilla. Heat in a double boiler while whisking. When the mixture is steaming add the cornstarch solution. Whisk continuously until well thickened to "mayonnaise" consistency. Remove from pan and let cool before refrigerating. Chill before using.

Other flavorings may also be used.

108 Buttercream Frosting

A very buttery, very creamy-smooth frosting, one we have used at our bakery. It works well for decorating and can be flavored in a variety of ways. This recipe is a lot of work without a mixer.

3 egg whites
1 cup sugar
2 tablespoons corn syrup
⅝ cup sweet butter, softened
flavoring: vanilla extract, Kahlua, or Grand Marnier

[Enough to layer and top an 8-inch cake]

Blend egg whites, sugar, and corn syrup together, and put in a double boiler to heat. Meanwhile, whip the butter until it is "white 'n' light." Heat the whites until they are too hot to touch and the sugar granules have dissolved. Then remove them from the heat and whip them until they turn marshmallow. While continuing to whip the whites, add the whipped butter a handful at a time. Season with vanilla, Kahlua, Grand Marnier, or other liqueur, or try a spot of lemon juice. Use immediately or keep refrigerated.

109 Cream Cheese Icing

We have used this on our carrot cake and other cakes. White and creamy, it also can be used for cake decorating.

8 ounces fresh cream cheese at room temperature
½ cup sweet butter at room temperature
3 cups powdered sugar
1 teaspoon vanilla extract
juice and zest of ½ lemon

[Icing for 1 large cake]

Cream together the cream cheese and butter. Slowly sift in the powdered sugar and beat until the mixture is well blended and has no lumps. Then stir in the vanilla and lemon.

110 Chocolate Mousse Pie

A dessert classic, chocolate mousse, juxtaposed with a chocolate crust, the creamy smoothness of the filling given a bed of crunchiness. Irresistible for chocolate-lovers. The recipe calls for making up a double batch of chocolate "cookies" which are to be made into crumbs for the pie shell. The double batch makes enough crumbs for two shells, so you will have some crumbs on hand for next time. Although it may look complicated, this mousse pie is surprisingly easy to prepare.

For 2 pie shells:

> 2 ounces unsweetened chocolate
> ¼ cup butter
> ½ cup sugar
> 1 egg
> 1 teaspoon vanilla extract
> 1 teaspoon milk
> 1½ cups unbleached white flour
> ¾ teaspoon baking powder
> ¼ teaspoon baking soda
> pinch salt
> ¼ cup melted butter per pie shell

[Preheat oven to 325°]

To prepare the pie shell:

Melt and stir the chocolate and butter over very low heat or in a double boiler. Remove from heat when melted. Pour into a bowl. Mix in the sugar, then blend in the egg, vanilla, and milk. Stir in the flour, along with the baking powder, soda, and salt.

Spread batter about ¼ inch thick on a greased baking sheet. Bake at 325° for 25 minutes. Remove from the oven and break into pieces about one-inch square. Continue baking another 15 minutes. Let cool. Make the pieces into crumbs by placing them in a zip-lock plastic bag and crumbling them with a rolling pin. This makes enough crumbs for two pies.

For each pie (about 1½ cups of crumbs), mix in ¼ cup of melted butter. (If you are making just one pie, store the other half of the crumbs in a closed container.) Press the buttered crumbs by hand into a 9-inch pie tin, evenly distributing them on the sides and bottom.

(continued)

For each mousse filling:

8 ounces semisweet chocolate
2 egg yolks
2 egg whites
1 whole egg
¼ cup sugar
1 cup whipping cream
¼ cup rum

To prepare the mousse filling and assemble the pie:

Melt the chocolate over a very low flame or in a double boiler. Heat slowly, just enough to melt, stirring some to help it along. Remove from heat. Separate two eggs. Combine the yolks with the whole egg. Beat the egg whites to soft peaks, then add the sugar and continue beating until stiff but not dry. In a separate bowl, whip the cream and add the rum to it. Whisk the egg and yolks and mix in the chocolate. Fold in the whipped cream one-third at a time. Fold in the whites. Fill the pie shell and smooth off the top. Refrigerate.

The pie may be decorated with rosettes of whipped cream if you have a pastry tube.

I I I Short Pastry for Tarts

Here are two recipes for tart crust, which can be used for Fresh Fruit Tarts, as a substitute for the chocolate crust in Chocolate Mousse Pie, or as a crust for other pastries of your choosing.

1½ cups unbleached white flour
¼ cup white sugar
pinch of salt, or to taste
1½ sticks sweet butter
2 egg yolks
1½ teaspoons vanilla extract
2 teaspoons cold water

[Makes 1 large crust]

Sift the dry ingredients together, and work in the butter until a mealy dough forms. Stir in the yolks, vanilla, and water, and form the dough into a ball, working briefly with your hands just until the flour is all incorporated. Wrap in plastic and chill thoroughly—at least 30 minutes.

Here is the other one, and then the directions for baking.

1½ cups unbleached white flour
2 tablespoons powdered sugar
¼ cup finely ground almonds
pinch of salt, or to taste
½ cup sweet butter, cut into small pieces
1 egg
2 tablespoons lemon juice (or water)

[Makes 1 crust]

Combine the flour, sugar, almonds, and salt. Work the butter into the dry mixture until it becomes mealy. Add the egg and lemon juice or water. Work together until the flour disappears and the dough no longer sticks to your hands. Place in a plastic bag and form into a ball and then into a disk 6–8 inches in diameter. Chill for at least 30 minutes.

To prepare the crust:

Remove the dough from the refrigerator and roll it out to fit an 8–10-inch tart pan with a false bottom. Place the dough in the pan, press it into the edges, and fill in any tears or gaps with some of the overlap. Prick all over with a fork. Cover with foil and line the foil with dried beans or peas. Bake in a 400° oven for 10 minutes and then remove the foil and beans. Use this for a partially baked shell, or return to the oven another 8–10 minutes to finish baking to a light golden brown.

112 Fresh Fruit Tart

Glazed fresh fruit on a thin layer of Vanilla Pastry Cream set in a tart shell: jewellike, luscious, creamy, sweet, buttery—I find fresh fruit tarts beautiful, delicious, and intensely satisfying. Another piece, please.

Short Pastry for Tarts (#111)
Vanilla Pastry Cream (#107)
fresh fruit (enough to layer the tart)
fruit jam

Make one of the Short Pastries and bake it to a light golden brown. Remove from the oven and let cool.

In the meantime, make up a batch of Vanilla Pastry Cream. Spread a layer of pastry cream over the bottom of the tart—about ¼ inch thick. (You will not need a whole batch of pastry cream; leftovers can be kept refrigerated.)

Arrange fresh fruit on top of the pastry cream. Berries are probably the best for this: strawberries, blueberries, raspberries, ollaliberries, blackberries. Kiwi, peeled and sliced, is excellent, as well as banana— diagonal slices are pretty. Peaches and nectarines need to be quite ripe, and peeled and sliced. Seedless grapes are good. Orange segments, removed from their little envelopes, are marvelous. You are on your own for selection and design. Some fruits are generally too hard to be used uncooked, but if you are imaginative you can try apples or pears.

To glaze the fruit: gently heat some fruit jam or preserves (of the same, similar, or contrasting fruit) until it is runny, and brush it over the fruit. Ready to appreciate and enjoy.

Variations: A simpler fruit tart can be made by brushing the heated jam or preserves on the baked tart crust, arranging the fresh fruit, and topping with more glaze.

Or line the bottom of a baked crust with sour cream flavored with vanilla and sweetened with sugar or honey. Then top with fruit and glaze.

Cream cheese can also be used to line the tart shell, thinned with milk or sour cream, sweetened with sugar or honey, flavored with vanilla and/or lemon peel. Then arrange the fresh fruit on top and brush with the glaze.

142

113 Fresh Fruit Cheesecake Tart

This recipe is good with fruits that can take some baking: apples, pears, apricots, peaches, possibly nectarines. Some of the berries are O.K. too, if you like them really soft. (You get the idea that I prefer the Fresh Fruit Tart for berries?)

1 tart shell, partially baked (see Short Pastry for Tarts, #111)
4 ounces cream cheese
2 tablespoons honey OR sugar
1 egg
¼ cup sour cream OR 2 tablespoons milk
¼ teaspoon vanilla extract
grated peel of ½ lemon
fresh fruit (enough to layer the tart)
fruit jam or preserves (apricot or raspberry are good if you cannot decide)

[Makes 1 tart
Preheat oven to 350°]

Make up and partially bake a Short Pastry for Tarts.

Meanwhile, soften the cream cheese with a mixing spoon, then blend in the sweetening, the egg, and then the sour cream or milk. Mix in the seasoning.

Pour the cream cheese mixture into the partially baked tart shell. Arrange the fresh fruit decoratively on top of the cream cheese. If using apples or pears, slice them thinly, and arrange in a slightly overlapping pattern. Apricots can be left halved. Peaches and nectarines are probably best peeled. (Plunge in boiling water for 10–15 seconds before peeling to loosen the skins.)

Heat some fruit jam or preserves (using the same, similar, or contrasting fruit) over a low flame until liquidy. Brush it on top of the fruit. Bake the tart at 350° for 20–25 minutes or until the fruit has softened and the cream cheese has firmed. Remove from the oven and repeat the glazing if you wish.

About Ed Brown

Writing about myself: pretty difficult. The whole book is about me, but here goes.

First came to Tassajara when it was still a resort, in May 1966. Got a job as the dishwasher, learned to make bread, soups, and scrub the floor. I could never understand the cooks. One of the cooks quit. Offered his job, I jumped right in over my head. Instantly I understood—in fact I acquired—cook's temperament. What a shock!

During that summer my friend Alan and I did zazen together. One time Suzuki Roshi came down with several students. "The first thing to do in setting up camp is to carry water and gather wood. Now we have carried water and gathered wood," he said.

The next spring I was suddenly head cook of a monastery. Twenty-two years old and about as sure of my position as a leaf which falls in the winter creek. Proceeded to do a lot of things which I didn't know how to do, learning firsthand, the blind leading the blind. Bumped my head quite a bit, and a few other people's heads also. The actual cooking, I discovered, was the easiest part of the job. I was head cook at Tassajara for three summers and two winters, until, being completely devoured, bones cast aside, I was finally exhausted of food.

Now I build stone walls, which is really not such heavy work after all.

. . . Fifteen years since that was written, and still wondering, after all, "What is the real work? How can we save ourselves, literally and spiritually?"

At the Zen Center in San Francisco, I have been guest manager, head of the meditation hall, head resident teacher, president, chairman of the board. (I find it a great irony: going to the mountains to attain true realization and becoming an executive officer in a huge "corporation.") At Greens, our restaurant in San Francisco, I have been busboy, dishwasher, waiter, host, cashier, floor manager, wine buyer, manager (another irony—everything but cook). At home I have been married, divorced, coupled, uncoupled, the father of a daughter, now twelve.

I want people to be happy. I want all beings to be happy. Not the happy of getting what you imagined wanting, but the happy of kind mind, joyful mind, big mind; the happy of a day of peace, a day of tending, of attending ("You have to be present to win!" Jack reminded us recently); the happy of being with, not being boss, of greeting, meeting, patience, warmth, generosity.

Presently I am in residence at Green Gulch Farm, Zen Center's meditation community near San Francisco.

July, 1985

Acknowledgments

Actually, the fact that this book has come into being is rather incomprehensible and mysterious. In compiling a cookbook to meet the numerous requests of students and guests, I originally chose to complete the project in stages, beginning with breads. Even so, this book has been more than two years in the making. In the meantime I decided to devote myself to working on cooks, rather than cookbooks, and I had rather despaired of seeing this book completed. Fortunately the project has had the help and encouragement of several other people.

I am particularly grateful to Katherine Thanas for her efforts as editor, typist, consultant, proofreader, analyst, and friend, and for her incorrigible good nature. "What does *this* mean?" she would tease.

I am also indebted to Alan Marlowe for his work as editor, throwing out the rubbish.

Love and thanks to:

Kent and Frances for their beautiful illustrations—the best part of the book.

Diane Di Prima for typing over many of the recipes, running off with the manuscript, and finally returning it.

Peter Schneider for his friendship in supplying advice and editors.

The Zen Center Board of Directors for taking an interest.

Elizabeth Williams for her wonderful encouragement and hospitality: "Get to work."

The Wolfs of Portola Valley for their good humor and persistent prodding, "Please teach."

Judy, Yvonne, Dick and Ginny, and so forth.

Bob and Anna Beck, for getting me started at Tassajara, "teaching me everything I know," as Anna puts it.

For the recipes themselves, I would like to acknowledge and thank the following people: Lynn Good, Loring Palmer, Clarke Mason, Alan Winter, Roovan ben Yuhmin, Sandy Hollister, Kobun Chino, Bill Lane, Bob Shuman, Jeff Sherman, Angie Runyon, Maureen or perhaps Madeleine, Connie, Sandy, Niels Holm, Mary Quagliata, Grandma Dite, and all the other people who have made manifest their love, working in the Fabulous Kitchens of Tassajara.

Lastly, my special thanks and blessings to Jimmy and Ray, my original cooking gurus.

May we all nourish each other.

EDWARD ESPE BROWN
May 30, 1970

About Tassajara

Tassajara is a valley not quite lost in the mountains: natural hot springs, creek, maple, oak, alder, sycamore, and bay, rocks and hills, yucca, sage, and manzanita, quietly changing with the flow of the season. It's now the site of Zen Mountain Center, the first Zen Buddhist monastery in the Americas. Located in Monterey County, California, Tassajara has been a hot springs resort for over 100 years. Zen Center of San Francisco purchased Tassajara in December, 1966. What was the bar became the meditation hall (which burned down in 1978).

Here at Tassajara fifty to sixty students, both men and women, practice zazen, the traditional Zen method of sitting meditation, and follow a daily routine which also includes services and lectures, meals, work, bathing, and sleep. The Center continues to accommodate guests during the summer months, May through September. Guests follow a schedule of three meals a day. Their job is to have a good time (after all, they are paying good money). Guest food has always been highly complimented, often with remarks like, "It's too good. I can't stop eating." Visitors are delighted that some form of homemade bread is served at every meal, and they purchase a thousand loaves a summer to take home with them.

Tassajara is a peaceful place, a safe place to unregulate, to "take off the blinders, and unpack the saddlebags," to make oneself at home with who one is. Settling into the depths. Falling right through the depths. Awakening in the moment. We labor to feed. Working together, we develop many possibilities, create recipes and a life with one another.

Zen Mountain Center's address is Tassajara Springs, Carmel Valley, CA 93924.